Fresh Ideas in
Dried Flowers

Fresh Ideas in
Dried Flowers

Terry L. Rye

NORTH LIGHT BOOKS
CINCINNATI, OHIO
www.artistsnetwork.com

FRESH IDEAS IN DRIED FLOWERS. Copyright © 2005 by Terry L. Rye. Manufactured in China. All rights reserved. No part of this book may be reproduced in any form or by any electronic or mechanical means including information storage and retrieval systems without permission in writing from the publisher, except by a reviewer, who may quote a brief passage in review. Published by North Light Books, an imprint of F+W Publications, Inc., 4700 East Galbraith Road, Cincinnati, Ohio 45236. (800) 289-0963. First edition.

09 08 07 06 05   5 4 3 2 1

Library of Congress Cataloging-in-Publication Division
Rye, Terry L.
    Fresh ideas in dried flowers / Terry Rye. -- 1st ed.
    p. cm.
    Includes index.
    ISBN 1-58180-569-1
    1. Dried flower arrangement. I. Title

SB449.3.D7R94 2004
745.92--dc22
                    2004050065

Editor: Krista Hamilton
Designer: Marissa Bowers
Layout Artist: Camille DeRhodes
Production Coordinator: Sara Dumford and Robin Richie
Photographer: Christine Polomsky and Al Parrish
Photo Stylist: Nancy Kuhl

Some photos in this book were shot on location at Burl Manor Bed & Breakfast, Lebanon, Ohio 513-934-0400

Metric Conversion Chart

TO CONVERT	TO	MULTIPLY BY
Inches	Centimeters	2.54
Centimeters	Inches	0.4
Feet	Centimeters	30.5
Centimeters	Feet	0.03
Yards	Meters	0.9
Meters	Yards	1.1
Sq. Inches	Sq. Centimeters	6.45
Sq. Centimeters	Sq. Inches	0.16
Sq. Feet	Sq. Meters	0.09
Sq. Meters	Sq. Feet	10.8
Sq. Yards	Sq. Meters	0.8
Sq. Meters	Sq. Yards	1.2
Pounds	Kilograms	0.45
Kilograms	Pounds	2.2
Ounces	Grams	28.3
Grams	Ounces	0.035

About the Author

TERRY RYE has a passion for flowers and the best job in the world—creating exceptionally beautiful floral designs. Since 1980, she has owned The Mariemont Florist in Cincinnati, Ohio. The Mariemont Florist has been featured in numerous floral publications, in the prestigious Cincinnati Flower Show, and is highly regarded as a distinguished Professional Florist. As a self-taught floral designer, Terry loves to share the joy of flower arranging with others through her series of floral how-to books and is a presenter on DIY Network, which is part of the HGTV family. She also has been featured in many special interest segments locally and nationally. Terry resides in Cincinnati, Ohio, with her husband, Doug Eisele, and daughters, Sarah and Trina.

Dedication

With lots of love, I dedicate this book to my lifetime dear friend Barb Brewer, for all the wonderful and endearing past, present and future memories we have together.

Acknowledgments

Many thanks to all the talented people in my business, The Mariemont Florist, for their support, dedication and contributions during the completion of this book. I want to especially thank Billie Taylor, Mark Behnken, Janet Thompson and Lisette LaGory. They are so creative and talented! It is a joy to work with them each and every day.

As always, I am grateful to be working with such an experienced, helpful, and fun group of individuals from F+W Publications. They are so instrumental in making my series of books a tremendous success. I appreciate the great job my editor, Krista Hamilton, has done in keeping this book on schedule. Her attention to detail and composition will make this book a great success. My friend and photographer, Christine Polomsky, has a keen ability to conceptualize photos that are clear and easy to understand. She makes the written step-by-step instructions come alive through her photography. My heartfelt thanks always go to Tricia Waddell, who has continued to believe in my creative abilities for great "how-to" books. And many thanks to all the other wonderful people behind the scenes that edit, compile, proofread, produce, design and sell the books.

I also want to thank all of the talented and creative people who have purchased my books and have made their own arrangements with a little help from me. These books would not be possible without you!

I am truly blessed with a talented staff, great publisher, wonderful friends, and an incredibly supportive, loving family, Doug, Sarah and Trina, who never let me lose sight of what is most important in life—loved ones.

Table of Contents

Introduction

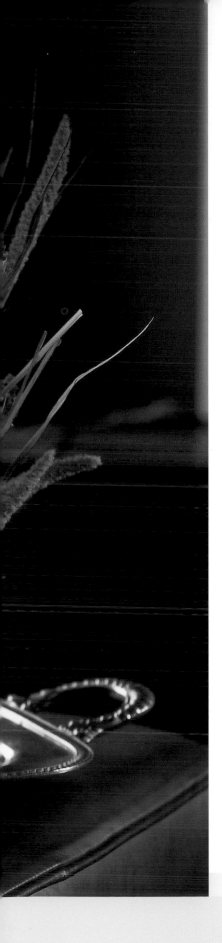

WHAT COULD BE MORE BEAUTIFUL than a fresh flower arrangement of lavender Australian daisies, yellow spray roses and purple hydrangeas? How about a long-lasting, dried arrangement of the very same flowers. Unlike fresh flowers, which have seasonal availability and wilt soon after being harvested, properly dried flowers will maintain their original color, shape and overall beauty for many seasons to come.

Imagine the feeling of planting seeds and nurturing them as they grow; watching them transform into colorful blooms; harvesting them at the height of their beauty; and preserving them so that they may be enjoyed from season to season. What a rewarding experience!

Within these pages, you will find twenty-two projects, plus variations and gift ideas, that will introduce you to the creative world of dried flowers. Whether you're harvesting and drying your own materials or using materials purchased from your local craft store, the easy, step-by-step instructions will teach you how to make a variety of colorful centerpieces, hanging arrangements, seasonal decorations and elegant gifts.

It is important to remember that arranging is not an exact science. Beauty is in the eye of the beholder, and your creations are expressions of you! So never give up, and most of all, have fun!

MATERIALS AND EQUIPMENT

Before you roll up your sleeves and begin making the beautiful dried flower arrangements on the pages that follow, you'll need to familiarize yourself with the basic materials and equipment. Everything listed below can be found at your local craft store.

ADHESIVES AND FASTENERS

Chenille stems – Similar to pipe cleaners, these are used to secure bows and strengthen flower stems. They consist of bendable, twisted, heavy gauge wire and a flocked material.

Craft glue – Craft glue can be substituted for most of the floral adhesives in this book to secure materials and supplies.

Floral adhesive – This is a dependable glue for wet or dry surfaces. It does not require heating and dries clear. For best results, add it to a surface and let it sit until it is tacky before adhering anything to it. Oasis is a common floral adhesive brand.

Floral anchors – Also called anchor pins, these are used to secure floral foam to containers. Floral anchors are used in Brilliance in a Basket on page 24.

Floral picks – Wooden floral picks come in various sizes, such as 3" (8cm) and 6" (15cm), and are available with and without wires. They are used to extend stem lengths, wire small clusters together and secure flowers and bows into foam.

Floral tape – This is used to wrap floral stems and bind flower clusters together. It is available in white, dark green and light green, and in various widths.

Floral wire – Floral wire is used to strengthen stems and bind flower clusters together. It is sold in a variety of gauges, and the lower the gauge, the heavier the wire. For the projects in this book, I used 18-gauge (heavy gauge) to wire thick flower stems and whole fruit, and 24-gauge (fine gauge) to wire delicate flowers and small pieces of fruit.

Greening pins – These pins, also known as S-pins, can be used as a substitution for floral picks when securing moss to the base.

Hot glue gun and glue – Perhaps the most important tool used in dried flower arranging, hot glue adheres flowers and other supplies to the base. It dries quickly and holds extremely well.

Spray adhesive – This aerosol spray works best on dry surfaces. Common spray adhesive brands include Elmer's Tack 2000 and FloraLock.

CUTTERS AND RULERS

Craft or paring knife – A good, sharp knife is handy for cutting stems at an angle and shaping floral foam.

Craft scissors – You'll need a sharp pair of scissors for cutting ribbon and thin stems.

Flower clippers – These are used for cutting medium to thick flower stems and branches.

Needle nose pliers – These are helpful for pushing stems into foam and dense arrangements.

Tape measure/ruler – These tools are used for measuring stem and ribbon lengths.

Wire cutters – Use these to cut thick stems and fine or heavy gauge floral wire.

Clockwise from bottom left: wire cutters; wooden floral picks; sand; moss; lemons; hot glue gun and glue sticks; floral foam; Styrofoam (various shapes); chenille stems; floral adhesive; paring knife; greening pins; floral wire; candles; candle adapters; and tape measure.

BASES AND HOLDERS

Baskets – Baskets made of wicker, wire, leaves and other materials make beautiful holders for dried flowers.

Containers – Jars, trays, pots and vases are available in tin, stoneware, ceramic and many other materials.

Floral foam – There are two types of floral foam: dry and wet. Dry foam, which we will use in this book, is used for dried and silk flower arrangements and is firmer than wet foam. Wet foam absorbs liquid to keep fresh flower stems moist.

Hanging holders – Decorative hanging holders are available in a variety of shapes and sizes and can be hung on walls, above fireplaces and on doors.

Moss – There are a variety of mosses available for use in dried floral arrangements, three of which are shown at the right. Feel free to use other types as well.

Sand – Use sand in the bottom of a container to add weight to a top-heavy arrangement. Sand is used in Buzzing with Beauty on page 48.

Topiaries – These are made of materials such as foam or twigs, and their shapes include single balls, double balls and cones. A ball twig topiary is used for the Sunflower Topiary on page 56.

Wreaths – Wreaths make wonderful hanging decorations, especially when adorned with dried flowers. The most common wreaths include grapevine wreaths, foam wreaths and manzanita wreaths (used in Manzanita Romance on page 70).

EMBELLISHMENTS

Beading – Beads are available pre-strung or you can buy your choice of colors and styles and string them yourself. They make make a beautiful addition to

Sheet moss is the most commonly used moss. It has a natural look and can be used in any arrangement.

Spanish moss is fibrous and grayish brown. It is best suited for arrangements with a gray cast to them.

Reindeer moss is the perfect accent to use along with other mosses, but it is rarely used by itself.

arrangements like Boxwood Tradition on page 96.

Candles – Available in many colors, sizes, styles and scents, candles brighten any arrangement. Just be careful with lit candles, as dried flowers can catch fire easily. I used candles in By the Fire on page 100.

Clear glaze – This product, available in gloss and matte finish, helps protect and preserve dried flowers.

Mulberry paper – This paper is available in a variety of colors, weights and textures. The edges feather easily when wet or torn, which you will see in A Palette of Color on page 82.

Ribbon – Ribbon adds flair to any project. Hundreds of styles are available, including grosgrain, double-sided, wired and satin.

Spray paint – A few light coats of spray paint will perk up the color or add bright accents to a dried flower arrangement. I prefer Just for Flowers brand spray paint.

Clockwise from top right: wicker basket; green and white foam wreaths; foam cone; mulberry paper; foam floral hugger; stoneware container; topiary form; and pottery container.

Getting Started

There are several methods for drying flowers, which are detailed below. When drying your own materials, always be sure to start with freshly cut, quality flowers and greenery with good colors and hearty blooms. For the most brilliant colors, the freeze-drying and silica gel methods work best, however the other methods also produce beautiful results. A brief list of flowers recommended for each method can be found on page 123.

PRESSING

Flowers with flat faces, such as pansies and geraniums, can easily be dried in a store-bought or homemade flower press. Place freshly cut flowers in single layers on newsprint or tissue paper. Cover the flowers with more paper and press between heavy objects such as books or bricks. Check the flowers periodically for dryness. Drying times vary, but this method usually takes about two to three weeks.

Flowers can also be heat-pressed with an iron. Place them between two pieces of waxed paper and press with a medium-hot iron. New pieces of waxed paper must by used for each pressing. This method preserves the flexibility and color of the flowers.

AIR-DRYING

Air-drying is the easiest and cheapest way to dry flowers. It is important to air-dry flowers immediately after picking them, otherwise they will wilt and the results will be undesirable.

Remove unwanted foliage from the stems of your flowers. (Detailed instructions will be given on page 21.) Gather the flowers into clusters and tie them together with string or an elastic band. Hang the clusters upside down from a wire or horizontal bar in a dry, dark and well-ventilated area such as an attic or closet. Damp places such as greenhouses, outbuildings and garages have too much moisture and will cause the flowers to mold. To speed up the drying process, hang the bundles over a broiler or dehumidifier.

Flowers with large, heavy heads can be difficult to dry upside down. Instead, dry them upright on a wire rack (shown at right). This process is often called open drying. Keep in mind that some flowers, such as roses and peonies, shrink somewhat when air-dried.

Allow the flowers to dry for at least one week, checking them periodically. When the flowers feel crisp but not overly dry, take them down and store them in an airtight container in a dry, dark place.

WATER-DRYING

This method of drying flowers will preserve their shape better than air-drying, but it takes quite a bit longer. Begin by removing excess foliage from the stems of your flowers. Fill a container one-quarter full of cold water and arrange the flowers in the container, spaced so that they are not touching. Store the container in a dry, dark and well-ventilated room. As the water evaporates, the flowers will slowly dry out. The entire process takes about three to four weeks.

Rather than hanging large flowers upside down, dry them upright on a wire rack as shown above. This is called open drying.

FREEZE-DRYING

Freeze-drying is another method of drying flowers and greenery. It requires the use of a freeze-drying machine (shown below). Although these machines are not readily available to the public, many companies provide freeze-drying services.

Fresh flowers are placed in vases or buckets containing water until they bloom into their ideal shape. The flowers are then dipped into liquid polymer, which is similar to liquid glue. This keeps the flowers intact and makes them pliable when dry. Next, the flowers are placed on trays and loaded into the main product chamber of the freeze-drying machine, where they are "flash frozen," or frozen at sub-zero temperatures. Once the flowers are thoroughly frozen, a vacuum pump is inserted into the product chamber to slowly extract water from the blooms. The water collects in a lower chamber of the machine.

The average drying cycle takes about two weeks, during which the temperature in the product chamber is slowly increased (but never above the freezing point). This allows the petals to release the moisture as they thaw. When all moisture from the flowers is collected in the lower chamber, the process is complete. Because the entire process is done below the freezing point, the flowers retain their shape and color when dried.

Freeze-dried flowers can be handled in the same way air-dried and silk flowers are handled, however the petals remain extremely porous and will reabsorb moisture. They should not be displayed or stored in humid areas.

Freeze-drying machines such as the ones shown above include a main product chamber, a vacuum pump and a lower chamber to collect condensation.

DRYING WITH GLYCERINE

Glycerine is a material used for drying flowers, and it is readily available in supermarkets and garden centers. As with the other drying methods, flowers should be preserved immediately after they are picked.

Start by mixing two parts boiling water with one part glycerine. Place the flowers in a jar and pour in 3" (8cm) of the mixture. Store the jar in a warm, dark and dry place for about three weeks. Check the flowers periodically, adding more mixture as the original liquid evaporates.

Flowers preserved with glycerine will maintain their color, and food coloring can be added to the mixture to create even more vibrant colors if desired.

DRYING WITH SILICA GEL

Silica gel is the most commonly used desiccant, which is a fine-grained material used to dry flowers by absorbing their moisture. This method is quicker than air-drying, water-drying or pressing, and the dried flowers keep their original shape and color. The name is misleading because this material is not a gel at all; it is granular. You can find it in any garden center or hardware store.

To begin the drying process, pour 1" (3cm) of silica gel into a container with a flat bottom. Position the flowers in the granules (place flat flowers such as daisies face down)

and sprinkle more granules over the flowers until they are completely covered. Allow the flowers to dry for about two days. Remove the flowers carefully, using a paintbrush to wipe away some of the granules if desired. Store the dried flowers in an airtight container. Return the granules to their container and save for future use.

MICROWAVE DRYING

Another economical way to dry flowers is in a microwave oven. This method works well in conjunction with silica gel and other desiccants, but is not recommended on its own. Flowers with thick petals, such as magnolias and hyacinths, do not dry well using the microwave method.

To begin, pour 1" (3cm) of silica gel into a microwave-safe container and place the flower heads into the gel. Pour spoonfuls of gel over the flowers and build up mounds of gel behind the petals to support them.

Microwave for about two minutes on a medium setting (300–350 watts) for 10 ounces (284g) of flowers. If you are unsure about microwave times, start with one minute and gradually increase the time until the desired results are achieved. Remove the container from the microwave and let it stand for 15–30 minutes before carefully removing the flowers.

DIFFERENT TYPES OF DRIED FLOWERS

PRESERVED WITH SILICA GEL
Silica gel preserves the natural colors and shapes of flowers. It can be used in the microwave for quick drying.

AIR-DRIED
Air-drying often darkens the colors and alters the shapes of flowers, giving them a very distinct look. Air-dried flowers are more durable and last longer than other dried flowers.

FREEZE-DRIED
The freeze-drying method is the most expensive, as it requires the use of a freeze-drying machine. The result is a dried flower that maintains its shape, color and texture.

DRYING FRUIT

Adding dried fruit such as apples, oranges and lemons to your arrangement will enhance its color and smell.

To dry citrus fruit, cut it into thin slices and place on a baking sheet. Place the baking sheet in the oven on a very low temperature. Check the fruit often and turn it occasionally so that both sides are dried equally. Whole fruit can be dried in the same manner.

To dry apples, soak several thin slices in a mixture of 1 ounce (28g) of salt and 1 pint (473ml) of water. Thread the fruit with string and hang it in a warm, dry place until it is completely dry.

The freeze-dried rose heads shown above are being wired for easy handling and insertion. (For detailed instructions, see "Wiring Flower Heads" on page 17.)

Keep unused dried materials in an airtight container away from light and humidity.

CARING FOR DRIED MATERIALS

Follow these tips to keep your dried flower arrangements as brilliant as the day they bloomed.

- Do not place over or near a heating or air conditioning vent.

- Do not place in direct sunlight.

- Do not place in areas of extreme moisture or humidity.

- Remove dust with a feather duster or hair dryer on a cool setting.

- Spray once a month with a dried flower preservative spray to prevent fading and shedding.

STORING DRIED MATERIALS

Make sure your flowers are completely dry before storing them. Line a container with tissue paper and layer the paper with dried flowers. Be sure to place heavier flowers on the bottom to avoid flattening more delicate ones. Place the lid on the container and seal it tightly. Store in a dry, dark place.

Basic Techniques

This section details some of the basic techniques of dried flower arranging that you will use throughout the book. Refer back to these pages if you run into questions along the way.

PREPARING A HOLDER

Before you can begin adding beautiful dried flowers to your arrangement, you must prepare the foam by covering it with moss.

COVER FOAM WITH MOSS

Place moss over the foam to cover it completely. You can use small scraps pieced together or a large sheet cut to the size of the foam. Hot glue the moss to the foam and press down gently to adhere, or use greening pins to secure the foam if desired.

Helpful Hint

Moss is a good filler for open spots in a light arrangement. If an arrangement is dense enough, however, moss may not be needed.

SECURING FLOWERS INTO FOAM

Fragile dried flower stems break easily with even the smallest amount of pressure, making it difficult to insert them into foam. The technique shown below will keep delicate stems intact and make the arranging process much easier.

1 PIERCE FOAM

Pierce a hole in the foam with a wooden floral pick.

2 REINFORCE AND INSERT STEM

Apply hot glue to the delicate stem to reinforce it, and insert the stem into the hole. Hold for a few seconds until the glue dries.

WIRING SMALL FLOWERS AND CLUSTERS

Tiny flowers tend to be overpowered by larger blooms in an arrangement. Adding wires to the stems, or wiring several clusters together to form a larger cluster, will allow even the smallest flowers to be seen in any arrangement. The size of the wired wooden floral pick you use will vary depending on the arrangement.

1 GATHER CLUSTERS

Group several small clusters together and hold the stems against a wired wooden floral pick.

2 TWIST WIRE AROUND STEMS

Tightly twist the wire around the stems and pick to secure them together.

3 WRAP WITH TAPE

Wrap the wired stems and pick with floral tape to secure.

WIRING FLOWER HEADS

Since flower heads have no stems, they must be secured to wire and wooden floral picks for easy insertion into arrangements. As shown below, heavy gauge floral wire and 6" (15cm) wooden floral picks work best for larger, more durable flower heads to give them more height and stability in an arrangement. In other arrangements, however, such as Manzanita Romance (page 70), fine gauge wire may be all that is needed.

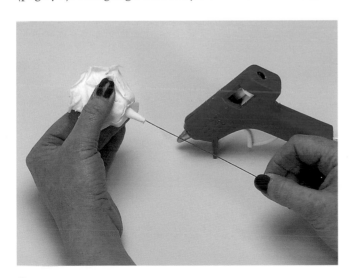 

1 INSERT AND SECURE WIRE

Insert a piece of wire up through the base of the flower and add a drop of hot glue to secure.

2 INSERT PICK AND WRAP WITH TAPE

Insert a wooden floral pick in the same manner as the wire. Twist the wire around the pick and wrap with floral tape to secure.

WIRING DELICATE FLOWERS

Securing delicate dried flowers such as hydrangeas to wooden floral picks takes a bit of finesse. Fine gauge floral wire should always be used with delicate flowers, as shown in the demonstration below. The size of the pick and length of the wire you use will vary depending on the arrangement.

1 INSERT WIRE

Insert a piece of fine gauge floral wire through the center of the flower cluster.

2 BEND DOWN WIRE ENDS

Gently bend both ends of the wire down until they are touching. Insert a wooden floral pick into the base of the cluster, resting against the wires. Do not twist the wires, as the flowers will be too fragile.

3 WRAP WITH FLORAL TAPE

Wrap floral tape around the wires and pick to secure.

WIRING DRIED FRUIT

In a few simple steps, you can add dried fruit to any arrangement. When wiring whole fruit, use heavy gauge floral wire as shown in this demonstration. For half or smaller fruit, use fine gauge floral wire.

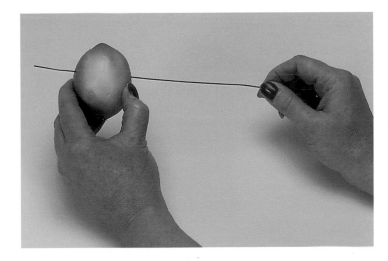

1 INSERT WIRE
Insert a piece of heavy gauge wire through the center of the fruit.

2 BEND DOWN WIRE ENDS
Bend both ends of the wire down until they are touching.

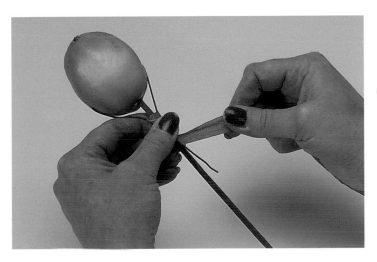

3 TWIST WIRE AND WRAP WITH TAPE
Insert a wooden floral pick into the base of the fruit and twist the wires around the pick. Wrap floral tape around the wires and pick to secure.

MAKING A BOW

Bows are often the finishing touch on dried flower centerpieces, hanging arrangements and topiaries. Follow these easy steps to make beautiful bows to complete your arrangements.

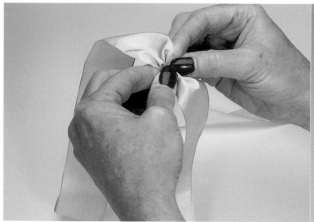

1 MAKE FIRST STREAMER

Keeping the ribbon on the bolt, pinch the ribbon between your fingers approximately 12" (30cm) from the end of the ribbon. This end piece of ribbon becomes the first streamer of the bow. If 12" (30cm) is not long enough, pinch further up the ribbon and make the streamer as long as you desire.

2 MAKE CENTER LOOP

To make the center loop of the bow, twist the ribbon with your fingers to form a small loop. Pinch the ribbon together in the center with your beginning streamer.

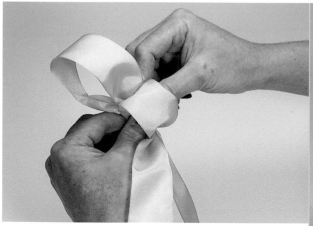

3 MAKE FIRST BOW LOOP

Continuing to hold the center loop, twist the leading part of your ribbon and make a larger loop, which is the start of your bow. The size of the loop will determine the bow's width. As you complete the loop, bring the ribbon back to the center loop.

4 MAKE ADDITIONAL LOOPS

Continue making loops from side to side until your bow is as full as desired. Four to five loops on a side is a common size. When you have made the desired amount of loops, continue holding the bow pinched with your fingers around the center. Cut your ribbon from the bolt, leaving a second streamer approximately the same length as your starting streamer in step 1.

NOTE: You must always twist the ribbon in the center before beginning a new loop.

5 SECURE WITH WIRE

Secure your bow by threading a piece of fine gauge floral wire through the center. Pull the wire evenly through the bow, bring the wire ends to the back of the bow and twist them tightly around the center of the bow.

6 FLUFF BOW

Spread out the loops of the bow and arrange the streamers so that they hang down at the bottom. To add more streamers, cut a piece of ribbon about double the length of the existing streamers. Pinch the center of the additional ribbon streamer and secure it with the wire holding the bow together. Adjust the loops attractively on both sides and trim the ends of the streamers with angled or V-cuts.

REMOVING UNWANTED FOLIAGE FROM STEMS

Flowers with sharp thorns, leaves and bristles pose even more of a threat when they are dried. To avoid accidents and prevent "sticky" situations, I suggest removing thorns, bristles and unwanted foliage from your flowers before drying them. When working with sharp materials, it is always helpful to wear garden gloves. Hold the flower with one hand. With the other hand, grab the stem where you want to begin stripping the foliage or thorns and pull downward on the stem tightly.

Thorns should be removed from roses (shown above) before drying to avoid "sticky" situations.

Plumosa (shown above) is thick with leaves that must be stripped before drying.

Classic Centerpieces

DECORATE YOUR DINING ROOM TABLE WITH A BEAUTIFUL CENTERPIECE MADE OF DRIED FLOWERS. Their brilliant colors and textures rival even the freshest flowers, but they will be around long after fresh flowers wilt away.

In this chapter, you will find centerpieces in a wide range of colors, styles and sizes. If you prefer bright colors, the reds, yellows and blues of Brilliance in a Basket will suit your fancy. If country is more your style, create the mood with Rural Reminiscence. If you like the scent of lavender, you will love the Heaven-Scent centerpiece.

You will also notice a variety of unique containers in this chapter and throughout the book. I love the playful quality of the decorative tin container in Buzzing with Beauty and the classic Victorian look of the Stoneware Victorian Centerpiece. The dark wicker basket in Oh So Rosy complements the lavender roses, and the black tray really makes the orange flowers pop in Reach for the Sky.

I hope you enjoy making the centerpieces in this chapter. Each one has its own unique style, and all are beautiful in their own way.

BRILLIANCE IN A BASKET

RURAL REMINISCENCE

OH SO ROSY

REACH FOR THE SKY

HEAVEN-SCENT

BRIMMING WITH COLOR

BUZZING WITH BEAUTY

STONEWARE VICTORIAN CENTERPIECE

SUNFLOWER TOPIARY

HYDRANGEAS AMONG US

Vivid color, definition in design

Brilliance in a Basket

This is a beautiful centerpiece with vivid colors and definition in design.

The arrangement would complement any kitchen table, coffee table or

buffet. The flowers are kept low for ease of conversation across a table.

The colors can be adapted to suit any décor.

MATERIALS

3 red balled mums [4"–5" (10cm–13cm) in diameter]

1 bunch (6 stems) of red spray roses

1 bunch of dyed red baby's breath

1 bunch of yellow tansy

2 bunches of yellow yarrow

2 bunches of lilac phalaris

1 bunch of dyed midnight blue yarrow

Sheet moss

14" (36cm) round basket

2 blocks of dry floral foam

2 floral anchors

3" (8cm) wired wooden floral picks

Flower clippers

Floral tape

Hot glue gun and glue

2 ADD SHEET MOSS

Completely cover the foam with sheet moss, adding hot glue to secure it. Visually divide the arrangement into three sections: red, yellow and blue.

1 SECURE FLORAL FOAM

Hot glue two floral anchors to the inside of the basket on opposite sides. Apply hot glue around the perimeter of the foam blocks and press them, glue-side down, onto the floral anchors inside the basket. If floral anchors are not available, secure with glue.

3 INSERT RED BALLED MUMS

Trim the stems of three red balled mums to 6" (15cm). Insert them in a triangular formation in the red section, avoiding the seam between the foam bricks. Position the center mum higher than the two near the rim of the basket and angle the lower mums slightly away from each other. Apply hot glue to the stems for extra hold.

4 ADD RED SPRAY ROSES

Trim the spray roses to 5"–7" (13cm–18cm). Insert them in a wedge shape to fill in between the mums.

5 ADD RED BABY'S BREATH

Trim the baby's breath stems to 5" (13cm) and gather them into small clusters. Attach the clusters to 3" (8cm) wired wooden floral picks. (For detailed instructions, see "Wiring Small Flowers and Clusters" on page 17.) Insert them randomly into the red section to fill in between the mums and spray roses.

6 ADD YELLOW TANSY

Trim the tansy stems to 5" (13cm) and gather them into small clusters. Attach them to 3" (8cm) wired wooden floral picks as in step 5. Insert the clusters of tansy into the yellow section, forming a triangle.

NOTE: Make sure the highest center flower is consistently the same height in each section of the arrangement. Keep the depths the same throughout the arrangement as well.

7 ADD YELLOW YARROW

Trim the yarrow stems to 5"–7" (13cm–18cm). Insert them into the yellow section, positioning one stem higher and in the center, and staggering the heights of the rest of the stems throughout the section.

8 ADD LILAC PHALARIS

Trim the lilac phalaris stems to 5" (13cm) and gather them into five small clusters. Attach the clusters to 3" (8cm) wired wooden floral picks as in step 5. Insert the clusters into the blue section.

9 ADD MIDNIGHT BLUE YARROW

Trim the midnight blue yarrow stems to 3"–4" (8cm–10cm). Secure them to 3" (8cm) wired wooden floral picks as in step 5. To finish the arrangement, insert the clusters randomly among the phalaris.

Delicate and abundant in blossoms

Rural Reminiscence

THE LAZY DAYS OF SUMMER MUST ALWAYS COME TO AN END, BUT THE ASSORTMENT OF SUMMER FIELD FLOWERS IN THIS COUNTRY BASKET WILL LAST FOR MANY SEASONS. THIS ARRANGEMENT IS DELICATE YET ABUNDANT IN BLOSSOMS. PLACE IT ON AN ENCLOSED PATIO OR PORCH FOR A TOUCH OF SUMMER ALL YEAR LONG.

MATERIALS

1 bunch of baby's breath

1 bunch of yellow rice flower

2 bunches of purple delphinium

2 bunches of pink larkspur

1 bunch of pink veronica

3 yellow ornamental flowers

3 yellow ornamental mums

2 bunches of basil millet

1 bunch of natural millet

6 stems of merlot chico choke

Sheet moss

13" (33cm) handled wicker basket

2 blocks of dry floral foam

3" (8cm) wired wooden floral picks

6" (15cm) wired wooden floral picks

6" (15cm) wooden floral picks (unwired)

Flower clippers

Floral tape

Hot glue gun and glue

1 PREPARE BASKET

Hot glue one block of dry floral foam to the bottom of the basket, aligning it horizontally with the handle. Place the second block of foam directly on top of the first block. Insert two 6" (15cm) wooden floral picks through the foam to secure them together.

2 INSERT SHEET MOSS AND BABY'S BREATH

Cover the foam and empty spaces on the sides of the basket with sheet moss and secure with hot glue. Trim the baby's breath stems to 8"–10" (20cm–25cm) and gather them into clusters. Attach the clusters to 3" (8cm) wired wooden floral picks. (For detailed instructions, see "Wiring Small Flowers and Clusters" on page 17.) Insert them randomly throughout the arrangement at the approximate height of the basket handle.

3 ADD RICE FLOWER

Trim the rice flower sprigs to 6"–7" (15cm -18cm) and gather them into small clusters. Attach the clusters to 3" (8cm) wired wooden floral picks as in step 2. Insert the clusters randomly into the foam at a lower height than the baby's breath.

4 ADD DELPHINIUM AND LARKSPUR

Trim the delphinium and larkspur stems to 10"–18" (25cm–46cm). Insert them randomly throughout the arrangement, placing the taller stems in the center. The height of these flowers should extend past the basket handle.

5 ADD VERONICA

Trim the veronica stems to 7"–10" (18cm–25cm) and gather them into small clusters. Attach the clusters to 6" (15cm) wired wooden floral picks in the same manner in which you attached the baby's breath to 3" (8cm) picks in step 2. Insert the clusters randomly throughout the base of the arrangement.

6 ADD ORNAMENTAL FLOWERS AND MUMS

Trim the stems of the ornamental flowers and mums to 10" (25cm). Insert them randomly throughout the arrangement.

7 ADD MILLET STEMS

Trim the basil millet and natural millet stems to 12"–18" (30cm–46cm). Insert them randomly throughout the arrangement.

8 ADD CHICO CHOKES

Trim two chico choke stems to 17" (43cm) and four to 12" (30cm). Insert the tall stems on either side of the handle, angling them outward at varying heights. To finish the arrangement, insert the remaining four stems randomly throughout the arrangement.

Warm, lush and romantic

Oh So Rosy

The dramatic jewel tones in this centerpiece will make a warm, lush statement for any room in your home. The velvet finish of the cockscomb add a romantic touch as well. You will see that the materials specify freeze-dried open rose heads, which produce the most vibrant colors of any drying method.

MATERIALS

1 bunch of lavender cockscomb

1 bunch of chartreuse cockscomb

1 bunch (10–12 stems) of sierra buds

1 bunch of sage yarrow

12 lavender freeze-dried open rose heads (no stems)

8 red freeze-dried open rose heads (no stems)

1 bunch of green hanging amaranthus

Sheet moss

10" (25cm) dark wicker basket

1 block of dry floral foam

3" (8cm) wired wooden floral picks

6" (15cm) wooden floral picks (unwired)

Heavy gauge floral wire

Flower clippers

Wire cutters

Floral tape

Hot glue gun and glue

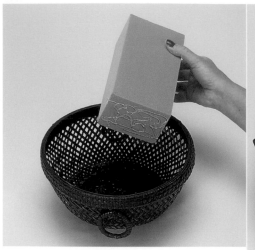

2 Add Sheet Moss

Cover and surround the floral foam with sheet moss. Make sure to fill the entire basket, tucking the moss around the sides.

1 Secure Dry Floral Foam

Apply hot glue to the bottom of the basket and one end of the floral foam. Stand the foam upright, glue-side down, and press down to secure it to the bottom of the basket.

3 Insert Cockscomb

Trim the lavender and chartreuse cockscomb to 2"–3" (5cm–8cm). Cut them at an angle to make them easier to insert into the foam. Insert the stems randomly into the foam, arranging the the shorter stems near the top of the arrangement. Make sure the colors are evenly distributed throughout the basket.

4 Add Additional Moss

Fill in the areas around the cockscomb with more sheet moss. There is no need to secure the moss with glue, since you will be inserting more stems into the arrangement later.

5 Add Sierra Bud Stems

Trim the sierra bud stems to 2" (5cm) for a total length, including flowers, of 7"–8" (18cm–20cm). Insert the sierra bud stems randomly throughout the arrangement.

6 ADD YARROW

Trim the yarrow stems to 5" (13cm) and gather them into clusters of three stems each. Attach the clusters to 3" (8cm) wired wooden floral picks. (For detailed instructions, see "Wiring Small Flowers and Clusters" on page 17.) Insert the yarrow clusters randomly throughout the arrangement.

7 ADD LAVENDER ROSE HEADS

Insert a 3" (8cm) piece of heavy gauge floral wire and a 6" (15cm) wooden floral pick into the base of each rose head to form stems. (For detailed instructions, see "Wiring Flower Heads" on page 17.) Insert the rose heads randomly throughout the arrangement, starting at the top.

8 ADD RED ROSE HEADS

To finish the arrangement, make stems for the red rose heads as you did in step 7 and insert them randomly throughout the arrangement. Since there are fewer red rose heads than lavender rose heads, insert them around the sides rather than the top.

9 ADD HANGING AMARANTHUS

Trim hanging amaranthus sprigs to 12" (30cm) and gather them into clusters. Attach the clusters to 3" (8cm) wired wooden floral picks as in step 6. Insert them randomly throughout the arrangement, pressing the picks deep into the foam. This will allow the sprigs to spill over the sides onto the table.

Picturesque Landscape

Reach for the Sky

THIS PICTURESQUE ARRANGEMENT CREATES A LANDSCAPE ALL ITS OWN. THE GRASS

AND FLOWERS SEEM TO BE GROWING RIGHT OUT OF THIS SPECIAL CONTAINER. THE USE

OF ORANGES, BROWNS AND GREENS WILL ENHANCE THE AUTUMN SEASON INDOORS.

MATERIALS

1–2 bunches of iris grass

1 bunch of orange Indian paintbrush

1 bunch of orange yarrow

1 bunch of orange marigolds

1 bunch of burnt orange Chinese millet

Sheet moss

10" x 13" (25cm x 33cm) black leaf tray

3 blocks of dry floral foam

Flower clippers

Hot glue gun and glue

1 SECURE FOAM AND ADD MOSS

Apply hot glue to the top of each foam block and place them glue-side down in the base of the tray. Press to secure. Cover the foam with sheet moss and use hot glue to secure.

2 INSERT IRIS GRASS STALKS

Trim the iris grass to 7" (18cm) from the bottom of the stems. Set the top portion of the grass, or the "tips," aside for use in step 3. Gather the bottom portion of the grass, or the "stalks," into clusters of two or three blades each. Insert the stalks randomly and at varying heights throughout the arrangement, starting at the center and working out to the edges to completely cover the inside of the tray.

3 ADD IRIS GRASS TIPS

Retrieve the tips from step 2. They should measure between 7"–16" (18cm–41cm) in height. Feather the ends by splitting them two or three times, about one-third of the way down. Gather them into clusters of two or three blades each and insert them randomly and at varying heights throughout the arrangement.

5 ADD YARROW

Trim the yarrow stems to 8" (20cm) and insert them randomly and at varying heights throughout the arrangement.

4 ADD INDIAN PAINTBRUSH

Trim the Indian paintbrush stems to 10" (25cm) and insert them randomly and at varying heights throughout the arrangement.

6 ADD MARIGOLDS AND MILLET

Trim the marigold stems to 10"–12" (25m–30cm) and insert them randomly throughout the arrangement. To finish the arrangement, trim half of the Chinese millet stems to 12" (30cm) and the other half to 8" (20cm). Position the taller stems in the center and shorter stems on the outside.

Sweet smelling, warm and inviting

Heaven-Scent

The clear glass container and lavender potpourri add a Victorian touch to this arrangement. Place this sweet smelling arrangement on your mantel or table and surround it with votives for a warm and inviting party decoration.

MATERIALS

3 large lavender exotic artichokes

3 green artichokes

6 stems of small pods

1 bunch of yellow spray roses

2–3 bunches of purple flowering oregano

1 bag of lavender potpourri

12" x 7¾" (30cm x 20cm) glass vase

8" (20cm) moss-covered floral foam ball

3" (8cm) wired wooden floral picks

Flower clippers

Craft or paring knife

Floral tape

Hot glue gun and glue

1 PREPARE VASE

Fill the vase with lavender potpourri. Using a knife, cut the foam ball in half. Hot glue one half, round-side up, to the rim of the vase.

2 INSERT LAVENDER EXOTIC ARTICHOKES

Trim the lavender exotic artichoke stems to 2" (5cm) from the base of the flower heads. Insert the artichokes in a triangular formation off-center in the middle of the arrangement. Secure the stems into the foam by making holes in the foam and adding a drop of hot glue to the end of each stem. (For detailed instructions, see "Securing Flowers into Foam" on page 16.)

3 ADD GREEN ARTICHOKES

Trim the green artichokes to 1" (3cm) from the base of the flower heads. Insert the artichokes in a triangular formation between the lavender artichokes, securing the stems into the foam as in step 2.

4 ADD PODS

Trim the small pods to 1" (3cm) from the base of the pod heads. Insert two pods off-center in the middle of the foam and the remaining four pods around the perimeter, securing them into the foam as you did in step 2.

5 ADD SPRAY ROSES

Trim the stems of the spray roses to 2" (5cm) and attach the stems to 3" (8cm) wired wooden floral picks. (For detailed instructions, see "Wiring Small Flowers and Clusters" on page 17.) Insert four roses into the center of the arrangement, angled outward. Insert the remaining roses randomly throughout the arrangement.

6 ADD FLOWERING OREGANO

To finish the arrangement, trim sprigs of flowering oregano to 1" (3cm) and attach them to 3" (8cm) wired wooden floral picks as in step 5. Insert them randomly throughout the arrangement to fill in any open space.

Delicate, soft and feminine

Brimming with Color

PLACE THIS DELICATE PASTEL ARRANGEMENT IN YOUR BEDROOM, POWDER ROOM OR READING ROOM FOR A SOFT, FEMININE LOOK. IT CAN ALSO BE GIVEN AS A GIFT FOR A BRIDAL OR BABY SHOWER.

MATERIALS

3 stems of green oak leaves

3 green hydrangeas

1 bunch of pink larkspur

2 dozen pink roses [4" (10cm) in diameter]

3 large pink stems of ornamental strawflower

5" (13cm) ginger jar made of floral foam

3 yards (3m) of ⅝" (2cm) grosgrain ribbon in spring moss

Dried flower preservative spray

3" (8cm) wired wooden floral picks

Flower clippers

Craft scissors

Floral tape

Hot glue gun and glue

1 ADHERE OAK LEAVES

Remove several oak leaves from the stems and hot glue them to the base of the foam ginger jar to cover it completely.

2 PREPARE HYDRANGEAS

Gather the hydrangeas into clusters and attach each cluster to a 3" (8cm) wired wooden floral pick as shown. (For detailed instructions, see "Wiring Small Flowers and Clusters" on page 17.)

Note: Because hydrangeas are so delicate, you may also wish to use fine gauge wire and wooden floral picks instead of wired picks. (For detailed instructions, see "Wiring Delicate Flowers" on page 18.)

3 ADD HYDRANGEAS

Insert one taller cluster of hydrangeas into the center of the jar. Add the remaining clusters around the perimeter until the arrangement is full, dense and round.

4 ADD LARKSPUR

Trim the larkspur stems to 6" (15cm) and gather them into clusters. Attach the clusters to 3" (8cm) wired wooden floral picks as in step 2. Insert the clusters randomly among the hydrangeas. Pieces that may appear too long will be trimmed in step 7.

5 ADD ROSES

Trim the rose stems to 4" (10cm) and attach them to 3" (8cm) wired wooden floral picks as you did in step 2. Insert the roses randomly among the larkspur. To ensure that the roses are visible, do not insert the picks all the way into the arrangement.

6 ADD ORNAMENTAL STRAWFLOWER STEMS

Trim the ornamental strawflower stems to 5" (13cm) and insert them evenly into the front and sides of the arrangement.

7 ADD RIBBON

To finish the arrangement, tie the ribbon around the neck of the jar. Trim any long stems to give the arrangement its shape. Spray the entire arrangement with dried flower preservative spray to protect it.

Decorative, light and airy

Buzzing with Beauty

THIS LARGE, NEUTRAL CENTERPIECE IS ARRANGED IN A TALL DECORATIVE TIN CONTAINER.
IT CAN BE PLACED ON THE FLOOR AS A ROOM ACCENT OR ON AN OVERSIZED SIDEBOARD
OR MANTEL. THE GRASSES GIVE A LIGHT AND AIRY FEEL TO A ROOM, AND USING A DIFFER-
ENT CONTAINER WILL ENHANCE THE ARRANGEMENT WITHOUT CHANGING THE DESIGN.

MATERIALS

1 bunch of sage leptospermum

1 bunch of basil Chinese millet

1 bunch of setaria

1 bunch of avena oats

½ bunch of green triticum wheat

1 bunch of phalaris

1 bunch of green nicoli eucalyptus

1 bunch of red Mediterranean oak leaves

12½" x 7½" (32cm x 19cm) tin container

1 quart of sand

2 blocks of dry floral foam

6" (15cm) wired wooden floral picks

Flower clippers

Craft or paring knife

Floral tape

Hot glue gun and glue

1 PREPARE CONTAINER

Pour enough sand into the container to weight it down [about 4" (10cm)]. Hold two blocks of floral foam together lengthwise. Using a knife, trim the foam to fit if necessary and outline the blocks with hot glue. Insert the blocks into the tin container, leaving about 1" (3cm) of the foam exposed at the top.

2 INSERT LEPTOSPERMUM

Strip any foliage from the bottom of the leptospermum and trim the sprigs to 12"–30" (30cm–76cm). There should be at least a 2" (5cm) stem left on each sprig. Insert the stems into the foam, starting in the center and working toward the perimeter, tallest to shortest.

3 ADD CHINESE MILLET AND SETARIA

Trim the Chinese millet and setaria to 18"–28" (46cm–71cm), including foliage. Insert the sprigs randomly, working back to front, with longer pieces in the center and shorter pieces around the perimeter, facing forward. Try to avoid placing too many long pieces in the front of the container.

NOTE: Setaria needs a little help with stability, so be sure to insert the stems at least 2" (5cm) into the foam.

4 ADD AVENA OAT STEMS

Insert the avena oat stems into the center of the arrangement, working front to back. This flower does not "hang" over the sides well, so keep the stems away from the perimeter.

5 ADD TRITICUM WHEAT

Trim the triticum wheat to 18"–20" (46cm–51cm) and strip the excess foliage from the bottom 2" (5cm) of the stems. Insert small clusters of about three pieces each into the center of the arrangement.

6 ADD PHALARIS

Trim the phalaris sprigs to 12"–28" (30cm–71cm) and gather into small clusters. Attach the clusters to 6" (15cm) wired wooden floral picks. (For detailed instructions, see "Wiring Small Flowers and Clusters" on page 17.) Insert shorter, fuller clusters into the front and sides, and thinner, longer clusters into the center and toward the back.

7 ADD NICOLI EUCALYPTUS

Insert the four longest sprigs of nicoli eucalyptus into the back center of the arrangement. There should be no long pieces hanging over the sides. Gather the rest of the nicoli eucalyptus sprigs into clusters and insert them around the perimeter of the container. This should look fairly thick and full.

8 ADD MEDITERRANEAN OAK LEAVES

To finish the arrangement, trim the Mediterranean oak leaves to 6"–12" (15cm–30cm). Add the leaves around the perimeter of the container.

Rich, beautiful color

Stoneware Victorian Centerpiece

THE CHOICE OF STONEWARE AS A CONTAINER FOR DRIED FLOWER ARRANGEMENTS

ENRICHES THE CLASSIC USE OF DRIED MATERIALS AND MAKES THE COLORS "POP."

THERE IS A HEAVIER APPEARANCE TO THIS SIMPLE, YET CREATIVE, ARRANGEMENT. THE

MATERIALS SPECIFY SILICA DRIED ROSE HEADS FOR THEIR BRIGHT AND BEAUTIFUL COLOR.

MATERIALS

1 bunch of white rice flower

1 bunch of spearmint

1 bunch of rose veronica

6 silica dried rose heads of each color: peach, raspberry and porcelana

Sheet moss (optional)

7" x 5½" (18cm x 14cm) stoneware container

1 block of dry floral foam

3" (8cm) wired wooden floral picks

6" (15cm) wired wooden floral picks

Flower clippers

Craft or paring knife

Floral tape

Hot glue gun and glue

Needle nose pliers

1 PREPARE CONTAINER

Using a knife, trim the block of dry floral foam to fit into the container and hot glue it into place. Slice off the top of the foam about $1/2$" (1cm) above the lip of the container. Cover it with sheet moss if desired.

2 INSERT RICE FLOWER

Trim sprigs of rice flower to 4"–6" (10cm–15cm). Insert the tallest sprigs in the center and the remaining sprigs randomly throughout the arrangement. Vary their heights and angle them outward from the center to create more fullness.

3 ADD SPEARMINT

Trim the longer sprigs of spearmint to 4"–8" (10cm–20cm). Gather the shorter sprigs into clusters and attach them to 3" (8cm) wired wooden floral picks. (For detailed instructions, see "Wiring Small Flowers and Clusters" on page 17.) Insert the tallest sprigs in the center and the shorter pieces and clusters randomly throughout the arrangement.

4 ADD VERONICA

Trim the veronica stems to 3"–6" (8cm–15cm) and randomly insert them throughout the arrangement with the tallest stems in the center. Attach shorter stems to 3" (8cm) wired wooden floral picks as in step 3 and insert them around the perimeter.

5 ADD ROSES

Pair some of the rose heads in sets of two in contrasting colors. Attach them to 6" (15cm) wired wooden floral picks in the same manner in which you attached the spearmint to 3" (8cm) picks in step 3. Attach the remaining roses to 3" (8cm) wired wooden floral picks. Insert the taller roses near the middle of the arrangement and the remaining roses at varying heights. Use needle nose pliers to help push the floral pick into the arrangement.

OLDEST PRESERVED FLOWER

With proper care and storage, your preserved flower arrangements may be around longer than you think. The British Museum displays a dried laurel Roman head-wreath that is over 2,000 years old!

Two thousand years may seem like a long life for a dried flower, but not compared to the oldest flower ever found. The remains of the oldest flowering plant were discovered in 2002, embedded in a slab of stone in northern China. The plant, called Archaefructus sinensis, or "ancient fruit of China," is believed to be at least 125 million years old. Scientists have gathered that the plant once stood 20" (51cm) high and grew from water. Traces of the roots, leaves and seeds were still intact.

While the odds of your dried flower arrangements lasting for 125 million years may be unlikely, arrangements that are well taken care of can last for many, many years.

Eye-catching autumn masterpiece

Sunflower Topiary

The yellow sunflowers with sierra blossoms and red pepperberry turn this classic topiary into an autumn masterpiece. The addition of the unique green and chartreuse albiflora creates an eye-catching assortment of dried materials. In the right location, this can be displayed year-round.

MATERIALS

- 15–20 sunflowers
- 1 bunch of green albiflora
- 1 bunch of chartreuse albiflora
- 1 bunch of chartreuse yarrow
- 1 bunch of yellow sierra buds
- 1 bunch of pepperberry
- Sheet moss
- 6" x 5" (15cm x 13cm) terra cotta pot
- 19" (48cm) twig topiary ball
- 1 block of dry floral foam
- Flower clippers
- Craft or paring knife
- Hot glue gun and glue

2 INSERT SUNFLOWERS

Hot glue sheet moss unevenly around the topiary base. Trim the sunflowers to 2" (5cm). Apply hot glue to the stems and insert them randomly throughout the topiary ball. Insert one stem into the topiary base.

1 SECURE FOAM AND TOPIARY

Using a knife, trim the floral foam to fit the terra cotta pot and hot glue it inside. Slice off the top of the foam so it is ¹/₂" (1cm) higher than the lip of the pot. Cover the twig topiary ball with sheet moss using a hot glue gun. Insert the topiary ball into the center of the foam base.

NOTE: Don't cover the ball too densely with moss or it will be difficult to insert any stems.

3 ADD ALBIFLORA

Trim the green and chartreuse albiflora stems to 1"–2" (3cm–5cm). Apply hot glue to the stems and insert them randomly throughout the topiary ball. Insert one green stem and one chartreuse stem, each in a different size, into the topiary base on opposite sides.

4 ADD YARROW

Trim the yarrow stems to 2"–4" (5cm–10cm). Apply hot glue to the stems and insert them randomly throughout the topiary ball. Insert a few stems into the topiary base.

5 ADD SIERRA BUDS

Trim the sierra bud stems to 1" (3cm). Apply hot glue to the stems and insert them randomly throughout the topiary ball. Insert a few buds into the topiary base.

6 ADD PEPPERBERRY

To finish the arrangement, trim the pepperberry into small clusters. Apply hot glue to the stems and insert them randomly throughout the topiary ball and into the topiary base.

Vivid larkspur, soft hydrangeas

Hydrangeas Among Us

THE VIVID PURPLE LARKSPUR AND HYDRANGEAS LOOK SENSATIONAL WITH THE

CONTRASTING BROWN ACCENTS OF THE PODS AND WILD GRASS. I LOVE HOW THE

PRICKLY TEXTURE OF THE PODS IS OFFSET BY THE SOFTNESS OF THE HYDRANGEAS.

MATERIALS

3 large purple hydrangeas

1 bunch of lavender Australian daisies

1 bunch of purple larkspur

1 bunch (7–10 sprigs) of burnt oak wild grass

1 bunch (15–20 sprigs) of assorted pods

12½" x 5" x 5" (32cm x 13cm x 13cm) white wash tin container

1 block of dry floral foam

6" (15cm) wooden floral picks (unwired)

Flower clippers

Hot glue gun and glue

Needle nose pliers (optional)

1 PREPARE CONTAINER AND INSERT HYDRANGEAS

Hot glue the dry floral foam into the base of the container. Insert two hydrangeas, angled away from each other, into the foam at each end. The hydrangeas should lie almost sideways.

2 INSERT REMAINING HYDRANGEA

Insert the third hydrangea into the center of the arrangement, pushing the stem deep into the foam.

3 ADD DAISIES

Trim the Australian daisy stems to 6"–7" (15cm–18cm). Insert them randomly among the hydrangeas. Use needle nose pliers to carefully hold the hydrangeas while inserting the daisies. The density of the hydrangeas will hold the daisy stems in place even though the stems do not reach the foam. Use the daisies to balance out the hydrangeas and fill in any open space.

4 ADD LARKSPUR

Trim the larkspur stems to 7"–9" (18cm–23cm). Insert them randomly throughout the arrangement. Use the larkspur to balance out the hydrangeas and fill in any open space as you did with the Australian daisies.

5 ADD WILD GRASS

Trim 7–10 sprigs of burnt oak wild grass to 12"–14" (30cm–36cm). Insert them throughout the center of the arrangement.

6 ADD PODS

Insert a 6" (15cm) wooden floral pick into the base of each pod and add a drop of hot glue to secure them. To finish the arrangement, insert the pods throughout the arrangement, arranging larger pods low and at various angles.

Hanging Arrangements

A BARE WALL, DOOR OR MANTEL IS LIKE A BLANK CANVAS. There are so many ways you can dress it up, and you are limited only by your imagination. The right dried flower arrangement will tie together the other design elements in the room, such as your favorite sofa, lamp or end table.

In this chapter, you will find seven hanging arrangements that will dress up any room in your home. The colorful wreaths in Through the Grapevine and Manzanita Romance will look lovely hanging on a door or over a fireplace. Or decorate a study with the rich color scheme in Rustic Retreat.

Don't limit yourself to working with dried flowers and foliage. As you will see in this chapter, dried fruits are just as beautiful and easy to use. The dried oranges, limes, pineapples and apples in the Country Kitchen arrangement will add charm to any kitchen.

I have also included a few special features, like Tricks of the Trade, Enhancing Your Décor, and Choosing the Proper Container. I hope that by sharing the knowledge that I have acquired throughout the years, you will develop the confidence to create beautiful dried flower arrangements now and in the future.

Varied texture, bold colors

Through the Grapevine

This decorative grapevine wreath is completely covered in dried flowers. It includes an abundance of varied textures and bold colors in a soft setting of green hydrangeas. Because it is relatively small in size, it can be used as a wall hanging, a door or mirror decoration or even a centerpiece.

MATERIALS

3–4 large green hydrangeas

1 bunch of echinops

2 bunches (6 stems per bunch) of burgundy cockscomb

1 bunch of mint

1 bunch of strawflower in assorted colors

1 stem of white statice sinuata

1 stem of blue statice sinuata

1 stem of yellow statice sinuata

1 bunch of yellow tansy

10" (25cm) grapevine wreath

1 yard (1m) of 1½" (4cm) wide double-sided ribbon in spring moss

Dried flower preservative spray

Heavy gauge floral wire

Flower clippers

Wire cutter

Craft scissors

Hot glue gun and glue

Letter opener (optional)

1 ATTACH RIBBON

Cut a 24" (61cm) length of ribbon and insert a 10" (25cm) piece of heavy gauge floral wire through one end. Bend both sides of the wire down until they meet. Use the wire to push the ribbon through the grapevines in the back of the wreath. Pull the ribbon halfway through, remove the wire and tie the ends of the ribbon together in a double knot 3" (8cm) from the top of the wreath. This ribbon loop will become your wreath hanger. Trim the ribbon ends to the desired length and finish off each end with a V-cut.

NOTE: You may also use a letter opener to push the ribbon through the thick grapevines.

2 INSERT HYDRANGEA BLOSSOMS

Cut large clusters of hydrangea blossoms from each stem and secure them to the wreath with hot glue. Completely cover the front and sides of the wreath. Spray the entire wreath with dried flower preservative spray to keep the blossoms from shattering.

3 ADD ECHINOPS

Trim the echinops stems to 1"–2" (3cm–5cm). Add hot glue to the stems and insert them randomly throughout the wreath.

4 ADD COCKSCOMB

Cut the cockscomb heads from their stems and glue them randomly on the wreath.

5 ADD MINT

Trim the mint stems to 1" (3cm) and glue them randomly throughout the wreath.

6 ADD STRAWFLOWER STEMS

Trim the strawflowers to 1" (3cm) and glue them randomly throughout the wreath.

7 ADD STATICE

Cut the flower clusters from the stems of the white, blue and yellow statice. Apply a line of hot glue along the backs of the clusters and glue them randomly throughout the wreath. Add one color at a time for better balance.

8 ADD TANSY

Cut the tansy into clusters, leaving very small stems. To finish the arrangement, glue the tansy clusters randomly throughout the wreath.

Romantic and fragrant

Manzanita Romance

THIS IS AN ABUNDANT WREATH OF BEAUTIFUL BLOSSOMS. THE WREATH, MADE OF
MANZANITA TWIGS, IS A ROMANTIC BACKDROP FOR THE SOFT GREEN HYDRANGEAS
AND THE JEWEL TONES OF PEONIES WITH ROSES. THE LAVENDER ALSO ADDS A HINT
OF FRAGRANCE.

MATERIALS

8–10 green hydrangeas

1 bunch (6 flowers) of pink peonies

1 bunch (5 flowers) of burgundy peonies

1 bunch of pink roses

8 pale yellow rose heads

8 burgundy rose heads

1 bunch of lavender

22"–25" (56cm–64cm) manzanita wreath

Just for Flowers spray paint in Wild Rose

1 green chenille stem

Heavy gauge floral wire

Flower clippers

Craft or paring knife

Wire cutters

Hot glue gun and glue

1 PAINT HYDRANGEAS

Spray the hydrangeas with Just for Flowers spray paint in Wild Rose. The color will vary with the number of coats. For subtle color, spray lightly. Apply more coats to some of the flowers for a more vivid color. It is nice to have a variety.

NOTE: Larger blossoms may need to be split in half and re-sprayed.

2 PREPARE WREATH HANGER

Turn the wreath face down and insert a chenille stem through the metal ring at the top. Twist the ends together. This will provide a hanging system.

3 INSERT HYDRANGEAS

Trim the stems of the painted hydrangeas and arrange them on the front side of the wreath. Alternate between darker and lighter shades of pink. Hot glue larger blossoms down first, and fill in the empty spaces with smaller ones using a generous amount of glue. Once a blossom has been glued down, don't pull it back up to reposition it. Some irregularity is fine.

4 ADD PEONIES

Trim the pink and burgundy peony stems to 2" (5cm). Apply hot glue to the stem and base of each flower before inserting it. Insert them randomly throughout the wreath. They will be more secure if the stems are placed slightly into the hydrangeas.

5 ADD ROSES

Trim the stems of the pink roses to 1"–2" (3cm–5cm), removing excess foliage. (For detailed instructions, see "Removing Unwanted Foliage from Stems" on page 21.) Apply hot glue to the stems and bases of the blossoms and insert them randomly among the hydrangeas.

6 ADD ROSE HEADS

Cut 16 pieces of heavy gauge floral wire to 3" (8cm) each. Insert a wire into the base of each yellow and burgundy rose head. Apply a dab of hot glue to the wire and base of each rose head to secure it to the wreath. Insert the rose heads into the hydrangeas, randomly alternating the colors for balance.

NOTE: If a rose is on the verge of falling apart, you can glue it into the arrangement without the wire.

7 ADD LAVENDER

Trim the lavender stems to 1" (3cm) and apply glue to the stems. To finish the arrangement, insert the lavender stems randomly throughout the wreath.

Stately, bold and masculine

Rustic Retreat

The stately design and color of this hanging arrangement are perfect for an office, study or reading room. The bold colors lend a masculine feel to the piece. I especially love the hanging wall tin in this arrangement, with its crackled brown finish.

4 brick red hydrangeas

½ bunch of ruscus

1 bunch of yellow setaria

½ bunch of yellow roses

½ bunch of salal foliage in various shades of gold

12" (30cm) crackled brown hanging flower holder

1 block of dry floral foam

3" (8cm) wired wooden floral picks

1 chenille stem

Flower clippers

Craft or paring knife

Floral tape

Hot glue gun and glue

1 INSERT FOAM AND HYDRANGEAS

Using a knife, trim the foam to fit into the holder and hot glue it in place. Trim any foam that sticks out of the holder, making it flush with the top. Attach a chenille stem to the back of the holder to use as a hanger. Trim the hydrangea stems to 1" (3cm) and gather them into small clusters. Attach the clusters to 3" (8cm) wired wooden floral picks. (For detailed instructions, see "Wiring Small Flowers and Clusters" on page 17.) Insert each cluster into the foam, covering the surface of the holder.

2 ADD RUSCUS

Trim the ruscus sprigs to 12"–15" (30cm–38cm) and insert them at varying heights into the back and center of the arrangement among the hydrangeas.

3 ADD SETARIA

Trim the setaria stems to 12"–18" (30m–46cm) and insert them toward the back of the arrangement in a horizontal row. Repeat with another row toward the front.

4 ADD ROSES

Trim the stems of the yellow roses to 6"–8" (15cm–20cm).
Remove the excess foliage and leave some stems with more than
one head. Attach them to 3" (8cm) wired wooden floral picks as
in step 1. Starting in the center, insert the stems among the
ruscus and setaria at varying heights. To add depth, insert some
of the roses toward the back and some toward the front.

5 ADD SALAL

Trim stems of several salal leaves to 10"–12" (25cm–30cm) and
attach them to 3" (8cm) wired wooden floral picks as in step 1.
To finish the arrangement, insert the stems into the center in a
triangular formation.

TRICKS OF THE TRADE

With over twenty years of floral arranging under my belt, I've learned a thing or two about working with dried flowers. I'd like to share my
knowledge with you. Here are some simple tricks that can be applied to any dried flower project. They will allow you to spend less time
arranging your flowers and more time enjoying them!

- If your flower holder is not flat on the bottom, place it in a
  larger vessel weighted with sand for ease while you work.

- To strengthen a hollow or unstable stem, insert a piece of
  heavy gauge floral wire through the middle of the stem.

- For an arrangement that is full and round, insert taller stems
  in the center and shorter stems around the perimeter.

- Use needle nose pliers to insert fragile materials into an
  arrangement to prevent breakage.

- If a floral pick breaks off in the foam, use needle nose pliers
  to pull it out.

- When attaching a cluster to a wired wooden floral pick, make
  sure the wire is through the thickest part of the stems.

- Try not to use a lot of glue on stems. It will inhibit them from
  going into the foam easily.

- Any drips of glue on a container can be easily removed with
  your fingers or a sharp tool when dried.

- After inserting a wired flower into a holder, bend the wire to
  change the flower's location if needed.

- Evenly distribute your colors throughout the arrangement for
  visual balance.

Real and natural, silver and sage

Pocket full of flowers

THE WINTRY LOOK OF THIS ARRANGEMENT IS SO REAL AND NATURAL. THE RED PEPPER

TREE BERRIES ARE A NICE CONTRAST TO THE SILVER AND SAGE SPRIGS OF EUCALYPTUS.

HANG IT ON YOUR FRONT DOOR OR MAILBOX TO BRIGHTEN UP THOSE SNOWY MONTHS.

MATERIALS

1 bunch of sage nicoli eucalyptus

8 sprigs of burgundy silver dollar eucalyptus

1 bunch of merlot Chinese millet

1 bunch of pepper tree foliage with berries

9" x 11½" (23cm x 29cm) green pocket tin wall hanging

1 block of dry floral foam

3" (8cm) wired wooden floral picks

6" (15cm) wooden floral pick (unwired)

Flower clippers

Craft or paring knife

Floral tape

Hot glue gun and glue

1 INSERT FOAM AND NICOLI EUCALYPTUS

Using a knife, cut the block of floral foam in half, lengthwise. Insert one half into the bottom of the hanger and the other half on top of the first half, trimming to fit if necessary. Fasten the blocks together with a 6" (15cm) wooden floral pick. Trim the eucalyptus sprigs to 12"–15" (30cm–38cm). Completely cover the foam with the sprigs and insert shorter pieces in the front and through the holes in the container.

NOTE: The nicoli eucalyptus should form your arrangement and be the base of all other material. This foliage creates a natural look.

2 ADD SILVER DOLLAR EUCALYPTUS

Trim the silver dollar eucalyptus sprigs to 12" (30cm). Insert them randomly throughout the arrangement at varying heights and angles.

3 ADD CHINESE MILLET

Trim the millet stems to 10"–14" (25cm–36cm) and gather them into six clusters of five stems each. Insert them randomly throughout the arrangement at varying heights and angles.

4 ADD PEPPER TREE FOLIAGE

Separate the pepper tree foliage into individual stems and attach 3" (8cm) wired wooden floral picks to any flimsy stems. (For detailed instructions, see "Wiring Small Flowers and Clusters" on page 17.) To finish the arrangement, insert the pepper tree stems randomly near the front perimeter to allow them to hang down.

ENHANCING YOUR DÉCOR

If you're looking for an easy and inexpensive way to rev up the decorations you already have in your home, dried flowers are the perfect solution. Here are a few ideas for how to enhance your own surroundings with just the right touch of dried materials.

- Re-energize an old ceramic container by adding dried roses in a variety of bright colors.
- Arrange a basket of dried summer field flowers such as larkspur, delphinium, statice and peonies and place it on your sun porch.
- Hang dried fruits, vegetables and herbs above the sink in your kitchen.
- Turn a plain terra cotta pot into a celebration of fall by adding dried grasses, wheat, cattails and yarrow.
- Fill a lackluster container with colorful dried blooms and tie matching ribbons around the top of the container.

Dried flower art

A Palette of Color

THIS FUN PIECE OF DRIED FLOWER ART CAN BE CUSTOMIZED TO MATCH YOUR DÉCOR.

MAKE SEVERAL AT A TIME AND GROUP THEM TOGETHER IN A HALLWAY TO ADD A FUN

ELEMENT OF DESIGN, OR GIVE THEM AS GIFTS FOR FRIENDS AND FAMILY.

MATERIALS

½ bunch of linum

1 bunch of burgundy peonies

1 bunch of yellow marigolds

11" x 14" (28cm x 36cm) pre-stretched canvas

8" x 11" (20cm x 28cm) blue mulberry paper

Just for Flowers spray paint in Fresh Green

6" (15cm) wooden floral picks (unwired)

Fine gauge floral wire

Flower clippers

Wire cutters

Spray adhesive

Hot glue gun and glue

1 PREPARE CANVAS

Spray the canvas with Just for Flowers spray paint in Fresh Green, making a background with an irregular amount of coverage. Allow to dry.

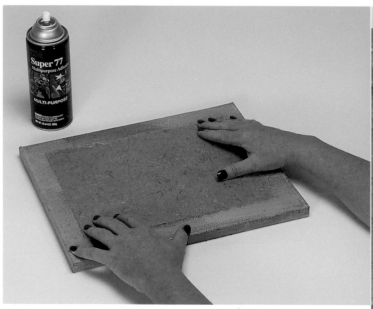

2 ADHERE MULBERRY PAPER

Tear the ends of the mulberry paper to feather the edges. Apply spray adhesive to one side of the paper and adhere it to the center of the painted canvas.

3 ADD LINUM HEDGE

Trim the linum to 7" (18cm). Place a linum "hedge" across the center of the paper and run a line of hot glue across the base of the stems. Allow the glue to seep down and adhere to the paper. Place a strip of fine gauge floral wire no longer than the hedge over the glued area at the base of the stems. Hold it down with two 6" (15cm) wooden floral picks until the glue sets.

4 ADD PEONIES

Trim peony stems to varying heights of 3"–6" (8cm–15cm) and adhere them with hot glue in the center of the hedge. Try to glue the stems to the paper, not just the linum. Some of the heads will need a spot of glue as well. Hold everything down while the glue dries. Insert smaller peony buds [as short as 2" (5cm)] where they fit in best.

5 ADHERE YELLOW MARIGOLDS

Snip the heads off the marigolds and apply hot glue to the base of the heads. Adhere them to the paper and stems in a row along the bottom, covering up the wire and glue for a finished look. Be sure not to go all the way to the edge of the paper. To finish the arrangement, trim any longer stems of linum from the bottom of the hedge.

CHOOSING THE PROPER CONTAINER

In most cases, containers used for holding fresh flower arrangements may also be used for dried arrangements. However, there are a few exceptions and additions that you may want to consider when choosing your container.

- Since the arrangement is dry, you are not limited to choosing a container that holds water. In fact, you are not limited to using a container at all! Decorate a picture frame, wall plaque or canvas like the one in this project.

- As you add more and more dried materials to an arrangement, it may become top heavy. With no water to weight down the container, the arrangement is likely to tip over. To prevent this, fill your container with sand or stones.

- I do not recommend using a clear glass vase to hold a dried flower arrangement, as it will expose the unsightly foam, wires and picks.

- Terra cotta and stoneware pots are relatively inexpensive and come in all sizes and colors. You can decorate them them with terra cotta markers as I have done in the Mini Healing Garden project on page 118.

- If you choose a container with a wide opening, be sure to cover the exposed foam, wires and picks with dried moss.

Autumn tones, assorted textures

Decorative Door Display

THIS DOOR DISPLAY IS ABUNDANT IN DRIED MATERIALS WITH AUTUMN TONES. THE ORNAMENTAL BALLS ARE THE FOCAL POINT, AND THEY ARE SURROUNDED BY AN ASSORTMENT OF TEXTURES AND TRAILING MATERIALS. THIS ARRANGEMENT CAN ALSO LIE FLAT AS A CENTERPIECE FOR A TABLE.

MATERIALS

1 bunch of basil long palm

1 bunch of terra cotta kunzea

6–8 sprigs of terra cotta hanging amaranthus

1 bunch of salignum female

1 bunch of green brunia albiflora

1 bunch of yellow yarrow

1 bunch of rust Mediterranean oak

½ bunch of green ruscus

Sheet moss

6" (15cm) decorative foam floral hugger

Three 3"–4" (8cm–10cm) foam accent balls

3" (8cm) wired wooden floral picks

6" (15cm) wired wooden floral picks

6" (15cm) wooden floral picks (unwired)

Flower clippers

Craft or paring knife

Stapler

Floral tape

Hot glue gun and glue

1 PREPARE HUGGER

Hot glue the sheet moss to the top and around the sides of the hugger. Don't worry about making it look perfect because it will be covered with flowers.

2 INSERT ACCENT BALLS

Insert 6" (15cm) wooden floral picks into each of the three accent balls, and insert the balls into the moss in a triangular formation. Leave a little space in between them.

3 ADD LONG PALM

Trim the long palm sprigs to 12"–15" (30cm–38cm) and gather them into two large clusters. Staple the sprigs in each cluster together, leaving them staggered at the top and trimming the ends even at the bottom. Attach each cluster to a 6" (15cm) wired wooden floral pick. (For detailed instructions, see "Wiring Small Flowers and Clusters" on page 17.) Insert one wired cluster into the top center of the arrangement and the other into the bottom center. Trim if necessary.

4 ADD KUNZEA STEMS

Trim the kunzea stems to 10"–15" (25cm–38cm) and strip excess foliage from the bottom 2" (5cm) of each stem. Insert longer stems into the top and bottom of the arrangement and shorter stems into the center.

5 ADD HANGING AMARANTHUS

Gather clusters of hanging amaranthus sprigs in varying lengths and attach them to 3" (8cm) wired wooden floral picks in the same manner in which you attached the long palm clusters to 6" (15cm) picks in step 3. Insert shorter sprigs into the center of the arrangement and longer sprigs into the bottom. Avoid using sprigs that are too heavy, as they will not drape properly.

6 ADD SALIGNUM

Trim two salignum sprigs to 12" (30cm) and the rest to 6"–11" (15cm–28cm). Arrange one 12" (30cm) sprig at the top of the arrangement and the other at the bottom, offset from one another. Continue inserting the sprigs, keeping them balanced from top to bottom. The shorter pieces will go around the sides and in the center.

7 ADD ALBIFLORA

Trim one heavier albiflora stem to 7" (18cm) and insert it into the center of the arrangement. Trim two more stems to 7" (18cm) each. Insert one stem in the upper left corner and the other in the lower left corner. Trim another albiflora stem to 9" (23cm) and insert it into the bottom center. Trim one last stem to 7" (18cm) and insert it into the top right corner.

8 ADD YARROW

Trim five yarrow stems to 7" (18cm). Insert one stem off-center and the other stems on each side of the accent balls. Trim the remaining stems to 12"–14" (30cm–36cm). Place the longest stems in the top and bottom center, and insert a few shorter stems off-center from those.

NOTE: For best results, try to end with one stem in the lower left, one in the upper right and one in the upper left. Refer to the photograph on page 86 for a better visual representation of this hanging arrangement.

9 ADD OAK LEAVES AND RUSCUS

Trim the Mediterranean oak leaves to 4"–6" (10cm–15cm) and insert them randomly into any bare spots in the center of the arrangement. Trim two or three ruscus sprigs to 11" (28cm) and the rest to 7" (18cm). To finish the arrangement, insert the longer sprigs into the bottom of the holder and the shorter sprigs randomly to fill in any open spots.

A little charm

Country Kitchen

This collection of citrus, pineapples, wild apples and foliage adds a little charm to the kitchen. They'll make the room smell great, too. Freeze-dried fruits are available in craft stores, where they are sold in bags of whole and sliced pieces, or you can dry them yourself as described on page 15.

MATERIALS

1 bunch of ornamental rice flower

1 bunch of green galax leaves

3 miniature pineapples

1 bag of red wild apples

1 bag of whole slit oranges

1 bag of green whole slit oranges

1 bag of orange slices

1 bag of apple slices

1 bag of lime slices

3 yards (3m) of 2" (5cm) wired ribbon in a fruit motif

Green chenille stems

6" (15cm) wooden floral picks (unwired)

Heavy gauge floral wire

Fine gauge floral wire

Flower clippers

Craft scissors

Wire cutters

Hot glue gun and glue

Needle nose pliers

2 WRAP WITH CHENILLE STEM

Wrap and twist another chenille stem around the entire cluster several times. Trim the extra chenille or wrap it around the cluster again.

1 SECURE BOW, RICE FLOWER AND PINEAPPLES

Begin by making a bow with 2 yards (2m) of wired ribbon and secure it with a green chenille stem. (For detailed instructions, see "Making a Bow" on pages 20–21.) Trim a cluster of ornamental rice flower to about 10" (25cm). Insert a 6" (15cm) wooden floral pick off-center into each of the three pineapples. Hold the pineapples together by the picks and arrange the rice flower cluster around them. Secure with the chenille stem on the bow. Use hot glue to secure the picks of the pineapples inside the bow.

3 MAKE SWAG

Tie the remaining ribbon around the base of the cluster and over the chenille stems, securing it in the back with a double knot. Tie the ribbon streamers into a loop with another double knot. This loop will be used for hanging the swag.

4 MAKE THREE DRIED FRUIT CLUSTERS

Strip the stems from the galax leaves. Thread a piece of heavy gauge floral wire with the leaves and dried fruit as desired. I threaded each cluster as follows: leaf, apple, orange slice, apple slice, leaf, lime, leaf, apple slice, apple, orange slice, leaf, orange, leaf, apple slice, orange slice and a final leaf. Bend the wire ends together as shown. Repeat to make two more dried fruit clusters.

5 ATTACH FIRST DRIED FRUIT CLUSTER

To attach the first cluster, thread one of the wire ends under the ribbon and through the chenille stem in the back. Then, bring the other wire around the other side of the swag and use needle nose pliers to twist the two wire ends together securely.

6 ATTACH REMAINING CLUSTERS

To attach additional fruit clusters, thread one of the wire ends through the middle of the first cluster and use needle nose pliers to twist the two wire ends together. Use wire cutters to cut off any excess wire.

7 ADD ORANGE SLICES

Cut three pieces of fine gauge floral wire to 10" (25cm) each. Thread five to eight orange slices onto each wire. To finish the arrangement, attach the wired orange slices at each intersection between the dried fruit clusters to cover up the connection points.

Seasonal favorites

AS THE SEASONS CHANGE, SO DO THE COLORS OF NATURE IN MANY PLACES AROUND THE WORLD. Fresh geraniums, larkspur and violets bloom in the spring, displaying a rainbow of greens, yellows, reds and blues. Summer brings the delicate blooms of hydrangeas and peonies. As temperatures fall, the leaves turn fiery shades of gold, orange and red during the autumn months. And nothing is prettier than holly and ivy in the chilly winter months.

I designed the dried flower arrangements in this chapter to capture the beauty of the seasons. Place the Boxwood Tradition centerpiece on your table to warm up the holidays, or decorate your mantel with the beautiful dried flowers and candles in By the Fire. A table wouldn't be complete without the Harvest Cornucopia, and who can resist gazing at the beautiful cut glass mosaic candleholder in the Springtime Mosaic arrangement? The Autumn Wheat Cluster stands up on its own and makes a wonderful accent in a hallway or the corner of a room. Winter, spring, summer or fall, these arrangements will capture each season the way Mother Nature intended.

BOXWOOD TRADITION

BY THE FIRE

HARVEST CORNUCOPIA

SPRINGTIME MOSAIC

AUTUMN WHEAT CLUSTER

Warm, elegant richness

Boxwood Tradition

Feel the warmth of the holidays with this elegant and formal boxwood tree. Using silver dollar lunaria as a sharp contrast to the dark green boxwood foliage makes this display very distinctive. The gold beading adds a richness to this arrangement as well.

MATERIALS

10 bunches of green boxwood

1 bunch of green hydrangeas

2 bunches of silver dollar lunaria

Reindeer moss

5½" x 9½" (14cm x 24cm) metallic ceramic container

6" x 12" (15cm x 30cm) topiary cone

1 block of dry floral foam

2 yards (2m) of 2½" (6cm) burgundy wired ribbon

8 yards (7m) of gold beading

Forest green craft paint

6" (15cm) wooden floral picks (unwired)

3" (8cm) wired wooden floral picks

Paintbrush

Flower clippers

Craft or paring knife

Floral tape

Hot glue gun and glue

Sand (optional)

2 ADD MOSS AND BOXWOOD
Hot glue reindeer moss on and around the base to completely cover the foam. Trim the boxwood sprigs to 2"–3" (5cm–8cm) and gather them into several clusters. Wire the clusters to 3" (8cm) wired wooden floral picks. (For detailed instructions, see "Wiring Small Flowers and Clusters" on page 17.) Insert the clusters into the topiary cone, working from top to bottom to cover the cone completely. The clusters must be inserted evenly around the topiary so as not to lose the cone shape.

1 PREPARE TOPIARY
Paint the stem of the topiary forest green. Use a knife to trim the floral foam to 2" x 5" (5cm x 13cm) and hot glue it into the bottom of the container. Wedge in a few extra pieces of foam to sturdy the base if necessary. Cut three 6" (15cm) wooden floral picks to $3\frac{1}{2}$" (9cm) and insert them in a triangular formation into the middle of the foam. Place the topiary cone securely on top of the picks.

NOTE: When choosing a container for your boxwood topiary tree, follow this general rule: $\frac{2}{3}$ tree, $\frac{1}{3}$ container. Weight the container down with sand if necessary.

3 ADD HYDRANGEAS
Gather small clusters of hydrangeas and wire them to 3" (8cm) wired wooden floral picks as in step 2. Insert them randomly deep into the boxwood and into the foam of the cone. Gently hold back the boxwood for easier insertion if necessary. Glue a few hydrangea blossoms around the base as well.

4 ADD SILVER DOLLAR LUNARIA

Trim the silver dollar lunaria to sprigs of two to five leaves each. Glue them randomly into the arrangement.

5 ADD BEADS AND BOW

Wrap the gold beading around the tree in swags, starting at the top. Secure the beads periodically with a dab of hot glue. Cut another 6" (15cm) wooden floral pick to 3½" (9cm) as in step 1. Make a bow and secure it to the pick with floral tape. (For detailed instructions, see "Making a Bow" on pages 20–21.) To finish the arrangement, insert the pick with the bow into the topiary base, through the moss.

ALL ABOUT BOXWOOD

Boxwood is a good plant material to use throughout the year for floral arrangements. It is often used as base greenery for holiday topiaries such as this one, which resembles a miniature Christmas tree. The clusters of small, dark green leaves will keep their color for months, or even years. Here are a few interesting facts about boxwood.

- Boxwood leaves retain their rich green color all year.

- Boxwood tolerates clipping well.

- Boxwood leaves produce red dye. The leaves are crushed and boiled in water until the desired color is achieved.

flowing and graceful

By the fire

This festive mantel display, complete with matching candles, will brighten up the holiday season. The spiral eucalyptus trails over the mantel for a flowing and graceful look. Change the color of the candles to gold or forest green for a slightly different treatment.

MATERIALS

1 bunch of ruscus

1 bunch of sage spiral eucalyptus

1 bunch of red sierra bud

1 bunch of red lin flower

10 birch branches

Small amount of sheet moss

2" x 8" (5cm x 20cm) Styrofoam weight form

Three 12" (30cm) burgundy pillar candles

3 candle adapters

Glitter gold spray paint

Dried flower preservative spray

3" (8cm) wired wooden floral picks

Flower clippers

Floral tape

Hot glue gun and glue

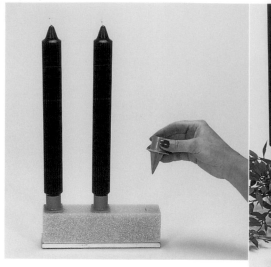

1 PREPARE CANDLE ADAPTERS

Assemble the Styrofoam weight form according to the manufacturers' instructions. Hot glue the candle adapters into the form, spacing them an equal distance apart. Place the candles inside the adapters.

2 INSERT RUSCUS

Trim a few ruscus sprigs to 3"–4" (8cm–10cm) and insert them into the foam around the candle adapters. Trim the remaining ruscus sprigs to 8"–14" (20cm–36cm). Insert them randomly into the top, sides and front of the foam at varied angles. Apply hot glue to any smooth stems to secure them.

3 ADD SPIRAL EUCALYPTUS

Trim the spiral eucalyptus sprigs to 8"–18" (20cm–46cm). Insert the longer sprigs near the bottom perimeter of the foam to hang down over the mantel. Insert the medium sprigs in the middle of the arrangement and the shorter sprigs at the top, angled away from the candles. Use hot glue to secure the stems if necessary.

4 ADD LIN FLOWER

Trim the lin flower sprigs to 6"–7" (15cm–18cm) and gather them into small clusters. Attach them to 3" (8cm) wired wooden floral picks. (For detailed instructions, see "Wiring Small Flowers and Clusters" on page 17.) Insert the clusters into the foam in an even row near the bottom and an uneven row near the top.

5 ADD SIERRA BUD

Gather small clusters of sierra buds and trim them to 8"–12" (20cm–30cm) clusters. Attach the clusters to 3" (8cm) wired wooden floral picks as in step 4. Spray the clusters with dried flower preservative spray and insert them carefully into the foam in a random fashion.

NOTE: Do not spray the entire arrangement with dried flower preservative, as it will eliminate the silver tone of the spiral eucalyptus.

6 PREPARE BIRCH BRANCHES

Trim five birch branches to 8"–10" (20cm–25cm) and five to 10"–14" (25cm–36cm). Spray them with a medium to heavy coat of glitter gold spray paint and allow to dry.

7 ADD BIRCH BRANCHES

Insert the longer birch branches as low as possible in a row along the bottom. Insert the shorter branches around the candles and in the center, applying glue to the ends if necessary.

8 ADD MOSS

To finish the arrangement, hot glue sections of moss to the back of the foam.

NOTE: Please use caution when lighting the candles in this arrangement, as dried materials are highly flammable. I recommend changing your candles often, before the flames get too close to the dried materials.

Bountiful and truly radiant

Harvest Cornucopia

Every table needs a bountiful centerpiece that captures the wonderful colors of the harvest. This cornucopia basket evokes a palette of radiant oranges with roses, Japanese lanterns and Indian paintbrush. The grasses and sea oats blend the harvest look together. I used pre-wired rose heads that were dried with silica gel to preserve their rich orange color.

MATERIALS

1 bunch of hedera arborea greenery

3 stems of orange Indian paintbrush

1 bunch of orange Japanese lanterns

½ bunch of green Congo grass

½ bunch of sea oats

½ bunch of yellow baby's breath

6 orange silica dried wired rose heads

15" (38cm) cornucopia basket

1 block of dry floral foam

3" (8cm) wired wooden floral picks

6" (15cm) wooden floral picks (unwired)

Flower clippers

Craft or paring knife

Floral tape

Hot glue gun and glue

Needle nose pliers (optional)

1 INSERT HEDERA ARBOREA

Using a knife, cut the foam block to 6" (15cm) long and trim it to fit inside the cornucopia. Apply hot glue to the inside perimeter of the cornucopia and the edges of the foam. Insert the foam securely. Trim the hedera arborea sprigs to 6"–8" (15cm–20cm). Insert them randomly throughout the foam with longer sprigs near the base of the cornucopia and shorter sprigs near the top. Make sure to add sprigs on the sides of the foam, too. This will fill in the gap between the cornucopia and foam.

2 ADD INDIAN PAINTBRUSH

Trim the Indian paintbrush stems to 8" (20cm). Insert the stems in a triangular formation with the heads angled outward.

3 ADD JAPANESE LANTERNS

Trim four Japanese lantern stems to 12"–15" (30cm–38cm) and insert them in a fan shape around the base of the cornucopia. Trim the remaining stems to 6" (15cm) and insert them randomly throughout the arrangement. Remember to insert a stem or two into the top of the cornucopia angled backward to add balance.

4 ADD CONGO GRASS

Trim the Congo grass tips to 8"–15" (20cm–38cm) and gather them into clusters of three to four sprigs each. Attach the clusters to 3" (8cm) wired wooden floral pick. (For detailed instructions, see "Wiring Small Flowers and Clusters" on page 17.) Insert the clusters in a semicircle along the base of the cornucopia, angled down so that the grass rests on the table.

5 ADD SEA OATS

Trim the sea oats to 6"–8" (15cm–20cm) and gather them into clusters of three to four stems each. Attach the clusters to 3" (8cm) wired wooden floral picks as in step 4. Insert the clusters randomly throughout the arrangement above the Congo grass.

6 ADD BABY'S BREATH

Trim the baby's breath stems to 4"–5" (10cm–13cm). Gather them into small clusters and attach to 3" (8cm) wired wooden floral picks as in step 4. Starting from the back of the cornucopia, insert the baby's breath clusters deep into the foam to fill in any open spaces.

7 ADD WIRED ROSE HEADS

Attach the wired rose heads to 6" (15cm) wooden floral picks by twisting the wire around the pick. Wrap with floral tape to secure. To finish the arrangement, insert the floral picks deep into the foam throughout the arrangement, using needle nose pliers in dense areas.

NOTE: If you cannot find wired rose heads, use regular rose heads and attach them to heavy gauge floral wire and wooden floral picks. (For detailed instructions, see "Wiring Flower Heads" on page 17.)

Airy, soft and feminine

Springtime Mosaic

THIS DELICATE ARRANGEMENT OVERFLOWS WITH COLOR AND STYLE. THE ROSES AND

PANSIES, CASPIA AND ADIANTUM FERN ADD AN AIRY, FEMININE TOUCH. I USED THE

AIR-DRIED PINK AND YELLOW ROSES IN THIS PIECE BECAUSE OF THEIR SOFT COLORS,

AND THE FREEZE-DRIED YELLOW ROSE HEADS FOR A BRIGHTER ACCENT.

MATERIALS

24 pansies

1 bunch of yellow air-dried roses

1 bunch of pink air-dried roses

6 yellow freeze-dried rose heads

1 bunch of green adiantum fern

1 bunch of caspia

Spanish moss

6" x 4" (15cm x 10cm) blue cut glass candleholder

1 block of white Styrofoam

3" (8cm) wired wooden floral picks

6" (15cm) wooden floral picks

Heavy gauge floral wire

Flower clippers

Craft scissors

Craft or paring knife

Wire cutters

Floral tape

Hot glue gun and glue

Needle nose pliers (optional)

1 PREPARE PANSIES

Place a pansy face down on a clean, soft surface. Use a 5" (13cm) piece of heavy gauge floral wire to carefully punch a small hole into the base of the flower. Apply hot glue to the end of the wire and reinsert it into the hole in the flower. Apply an additional drop of glue around the hole. Repeat with the remaining pansies, spray them with clear glaze if desired and set them aside to dry.

2 PREPARE CANDLEHOLDER

Using a knife, trim a block of white Styrofoam to 2" x 4" (5cm x 10cm) or the diameter of the candleholder's opening. Apply hot glue along the bottom edge of the Styrofoam and around the inside rim of the candleholder. Insert the Styrofoam about $^1/_2$" (1cm) into the candleholder. Apply hot glue to the outside of the Styrofoam and attach enough Spanish moss to cover it. Trim the moss with craft scissors if necessary.

3 PREPARE AND ADD AIR-DRIED ROSES

Trim the stems of the air-dried yellow and pink roses to 3" (8cm) and gather them into clusters of three buds each, keeping like colors together. Attach the clusters to 3" (8cm) wired wooden floral picks. (For detailed instructions, see "Wiring Small Flowers and Clusters" on page 17.) Insert the clusters into the Styrofoam at even heights, alternating between pink and yellow and creating a dome shape.

4 INSERT FREEZE-DRIED ROSES

Insert a 5" (13cm) piece of heavy gauge floral wire and a 6" (15cm) wooden floral pick into the base of each rose head to form stems. (For detailed instructions, see "Wiring Flower Heads" on page 17.) Insert the rose heads into the Styrofoam, using needle nose pliers and a drop of hot glue if necessary. Distribute them as evenly as possible.

5 INSERT FERN STEMS

Trim the fern stems to 3"–5" (8m–13cm). Separate them into clusters and attach them to 2" (5cm) pieces of heavy gauge floral wire. Wrap with floral tape to secure. Insert the fern clusters randomly throughout the arrangement.

6 ADD CASPIA

Trim the caspia stems to 2"–3" (5cm–8cm) and gather them into several clusters. Attach them to 2" (5cm) pieces of wire as in step 5. Insert the clusters randomly to fill in any open spaces, beginning in the center and working toward the perimeter.

7 ADD PANSIES

Insert the pansies from step 1, spacing them as evenly as possible. Use needle nose pliers to bend the wires if they are sticking up too straight. Snip off any caspia or fern stems that detract from the arrangement's overall shape. To finish the arrangement, spray the entire bouquet with another coating of clear glaze.

NOTE: Due to the delicate nature of pansies, especially when freeze-dried, this arrangement does not do well in areas of high humidity.

freestanding, decorative and striking

Autumn Wheat Cluster

This cluster of decorative grasses, sea oats and myrtle can be placed throughout your home. It stands freely and looks great in a corner or when grouped with a second cluster. The red ti tree adds a striking bit of color to complement the neutral surroundings. The color of ribbon can be changed to represent the season.

MATERIALS

1 bunch of meadow grass

1 bunch of dune grass

1 bunch of mountain grass

½ bunch of myrtle

½ bunch of sea oats

1 bunch of red ti tree

4½ yards (4m) of 1½" (4cm) wide wired red ribbon

Green chenille stems

Elastic band

12" (30cm) wooden floral picks (unwired)

Flower clippers

Craft scissors

Hot glue gun and glue

1 PREPARE THE MEADOW GRASS

Wrap an elastic band around one end of the meadow grass. (Store-bought grass may already be wrapped). Hold the bunch in one hand and use the other hand to slide the elastic band down to about one-third from the bottom. Twist the bunch slightly to fan out the grass on either end. Insert eight 12" (30cm) wooden floral picks up from the bottom and through the elastic band to add more support. Make sure all the picks are level so the grass stands up on its own.

2 ADD DUNE GRASS

Make an extra-long chenille stem by twisting two chenille stems together end to end. Place the dune grass bunch on your work surface, and place the meadow grass bunch on top of it. Slide the chenille stem under the pile and wrap the dune grass around the meadow grass at the same point where the elastic band holds the meadow grass bunch. Twist the chenille stem ends together tightly to secure the arrangement. Trim the ends of the dune grass at the base if necessary. Stand the bunch up and spread out the grasses.

3 ADD MOUNTAIN GRASS

Insert the mountain grass stems into the arrangement at varying heights, applying hot glue to the stems to secure them if necessary.

4 ADD MYRTLE

Trim the myrtle sprigs to 22" (56cm). Insert them randomly at varying heights throughout the arrangement, applying hot glue to the stems to secure them if necessary.

5 ADD SEA OATS

Gather the sea oats into clusters. Insert them randomly throughout the arrangement, applying hot glue to the stems to secure them if necessary.

6 ADD TI TREE STEMS

Insert the ti tree stems randomly throughout the arrangement, applying hot glue to the stems to secure them if necessary.

7 ADD RIBBON AND BOW

Make another extra-long chenille stem as you did in step 2. Use the wired ribbon to make a bow and secure it with the extra-long chenille stem. (For detailed instructions, see "Making a Bow" on pages 20–21.) Wrap the bow around the entire arrangement and trim the chenille stem in the back. Cut another 30" (76cm) of the ribbon to wrap around from the back to hide the chenille stem. Tie the ribbon in a knot in the front, positioning it under the bow and allowing the streamers to hang down. To finish the arrangement, cut the ends of the ribbon at an angle or in a V-cut.

GALLERY OF GIFTS

The perfect gift can't always be found at the mall or in a catalog. Certain people require the special, meaningful tokens of appreciation only found in handmade creations. Here are seven gifts made with dried materials that are sure to delight lucky recipients.

Decorative Urn

The vibrant reds, purples and greens complement the neutral color of the wheat stems in this decorative urn.

MATERIALS

6 dark green galax leaves

8 stems of wheat

7 large freeze-dried red roses

24 red spray roses

½ bunch of purple statice

5" x 3" (13cm x 8cm) decorative urn

3" (8cm) floral foam ball

3" (8cm) wooden floral picks (unwired)

Floral tape

Hot glue gun and glue

1 Hot glue the floral foam ball into the urn.

2 Glue the galax leaves to the ball, overlapping the leaves to cover it completely.

3 Gather the wheat stems together with a 3" (8cm) wooden floral pick. Wrap with floral tape to secure.

4 Insert the pick into the center of the ball.

5 Cut the stems of the large freeze-dried roses, spray roses and statice to 1" (3cm).

6 Insert the freeze-dried roses around the perimeter of the urn. Insert the statice and spray roses randomly throughout the arrangement.

Raspberry Rose Plaque

Give this plaque as a gift to a co-worker or hang it in your office at home or work. The floral motif adds life and energy to bare walls.

MATERIALS

13–15 dark green galax leaves

1 stem of green miniature oak leaves

1 stem of gray-green silver dollar eucalyptus

2 stems of periwinkle blue statice

1 raspberry rose head

4 stems of raspberry amaranthus

13" x 8" (33cm x 20cm) wooden plaque

Hot glue gun and glue

1 Hot glue the galax leaves to the edges of the plaque, overlapping them as you go.

2 Make a second row using the miniature oak leaves, working inward as you go.

3 Continue with a third row using eucalyptus leaves.

4 Cut the stems from the statice and glue the blossoms in a circle in the center of the plaque, leaving a hole in the middle.

5 Glue the raspberry rose over the hole in the center of the of statice.

6 Glue two sprigs of amaranthus on each side of the rose, positioned at an angle.

NOTE: To prevent the glue from showing through, apply it only to the base of the leaves.

GALLERY OF GIFTS

Mini Healing Garden

Give the gift of health with this spicy, aromatic arrangement. Known for its healing powers, sage gets its name from the Latin word *salvus*, which means "safe."

MATERIALS

1 bunch of dried sage

3" (8cm) terra cotta pot

1 yard (1m) of raffia

Pencil

Terra cotta markers, black and green

Elastic band

Hot glue gun and glue

1 Print the word "Sage" on the lip of the terra cotta pot lightly in pencil. Trace over it with a black terra cotta marker.

2 Draw leaf designs on each side of the word. Trace them with a green marker.

3 Gather a 3" (8cm) cluster of sage in your hand and bind the bottom with an elastic band.

4 Place the sage cluster into the pot.

5 Tie a piece of raffia around the base of the sage cluster in a simple bow.

6 Hot glue the center of the bow to the sage stems to keep it in place above the decorations you have drawn on the pot.

Keepsake Box

Decorate this tiny wooden box with beautiful flowers and share it with someone special. Imagine all the secret treasures that will be held inside!

MATERIALS

2 stems of green miniature oak leaves

2 stems of bay laurel leaves

2 stems of sea oats

4 blooms of dark pink amaranthus

4" x 5" (10cm x 13cm) wooden box with lid

1½ yards (1m) of 1½ (4cm) wide grosgrain ribbon in spring moss

Burgundy and cinnabar spray paint

Flower clippers

Craft scissors

Hot glue gun and glue

1 Spray paint the interior of the box with both colors.

2 Hot glue the miniature oak leaves to the lid's interior, overlapping as you go.

3 Glue the bay laurel leaves to the outside of the box, overlapping and folding around the edges as you go. Trim the excess leaves from the edges of the box.

4 Wrap the ribbon around the box, going down one side, along the bottom and up the other side. Trim off the excess. Fold the ribbon edges under and secure the ribbon to the box with hot glue. Wrap the remaining ribbon around the lid and trim off the excess. Fold the edges under and glue the ribbon to the lid.

5 Glue the remaining ribbon to the lid in the center, and fold the ribbon back and forth to make a simple bow. Glue the loops to hold them in place.

6 Glue a row of sea oat heads along both sides of the ribbon on the box and lid.

7 Trim and glue the amaranthus on each side of the sea oat heads.

Shadowbox Frame

Deck the walls with this three-dimensional piece of artwork. You can change the look to match any décor by substituting this mat for a ready-made mat, or by having a framer cut one for you.

MATERIALS

9 red miniature spray roses

12 red sierra buds

11" x 14" (28cm x 36cm) shadow-box frame

2 yards (2m) of 1½" (4cm) wide double satin ribbon in cream

2 yards (2m) of 1½" (4cm) wide double satin ribbon in spring moss

Craft scissors

Hot glue gun and glue

1 Remove the cardboard box and glass from the frame and unfold the box edges.

2 Cut six 12" (30cm) pieces of each ribbon.

3 Weave the ribbons together to make a mat.

4 Glue the ends of the mat to the box to secure.

5 Refold the box edges over the top of the ribbon mat.

6 Hot glue the roses and sierra buds at the intersections of the ribbons in an alternating pattern.

7 Clean the glass and place it over the mat.

8 Place the glass and the box back into the frame.

Glass Ornament

Make several ornaments at a time and give them as holiday gifts for family and friends. Be sure to make a few extras for your own tree as well.

MATERIALS

1 stem (about 26 burgundy leaves) of silver dollar eucalyptus

1 stem (about 40 florets) of hydrangea

Clear glass ball ornament

1 yard (3m) of ⅝" (2cm) wide sheer ribbon in light green

Flower clippers

Hot glue gun and glue

1 Remove the cap from the top of the ornament.

2 Remove the silver dollar eucalyptus leaves from the stem and glue them onto the ornament, overlapping the leaves to completely cover it.

3 Replace the cap on the ornament and glue it in place.

4 Glue one half of the hydrangea florets in a staggered pattern around the top half of the ornament. Glue the other half below of the first half to achieve a fuller look.

5 Cut a piece of ribbon and string a loop of ribbon through the top of the ornament. Knot as a hanger. Use the rest of the ribbon to make a bow and tie it to the top of the ornament. (For detailed instructions, see "Making a Bow" on pages 20–21.)

Rose and Hydrangea Wreath

Rose heads and hydrangea florets make this wreath the perfect embellishment for any door or wall. Choose different colors for the rose heads and ribbons to make a wreath for winter, spring, summer and fall.

MATERIALS

3 stems of green hydrangea and broken florets

20 rose heads in various colors

10" (25cm) floral foam wreath

Plastic sheet

3 yards (3m) of 1½" (4cm) wide sheer peach ribbon

Spray adhesive

Fine gauge floral wire

3" (8cm) wooden floral pick (unwired)

Floral tape

Hot glue gun and glue

1 Apply a coat of spray adhesive to the wreath.

2 Place the wreath on a sheet of plastic and sprinkle broken hydrangea florets over it. Apply the florets generously to the interior of the wreath and sparingly around the outside edges.

3 Secure the broken florets with hot glue.

4 Alternate colored roses around the wreath, gluing them in place to secure.

5 Make a bow with three sets of streamers. (For detailed instructions, see "Making a Bow" on pages 20–21.)

6 Thread a piece of fine gauge floral wire through the bow and twist the wire around a 3" (8cm) wooden floral pick. Wrap with floral tape to secure.

7 Tie up two streamers to make a loop. Knot the ends.

8 Insert the wooden floral pick into the top of the wreath and add a dab of glue to secure.

Flower Drying Guide

Not all flowers respond well to all techniques. Here is a list of the best flowers for each drying method.

PRESSING	Aster • Buttercup • Chrysanthemum • Dogwood Geranium • Larkspur • Lily of the Valley • Marigold Pansy • Poppy • Rose • Violet • Zinnia
AIR-DRYING	Baby's breath • Cattails • Celosia • Goldenrod Heather • Pussy willow • Rose • Statice
WATER-DRYING	Bells-of-Ireland • Celosia • Hydrangea • Yarrow
FREEZE-DRYING	Calla lily • Daisy • Gardenia • Pompon mum Stephanotis • Tulip
DRYING WITH GLYCERINE	Beech • Boxwood • Camellia • Eucalyptus • Ivy Magnolia • Mistletoe • Oak • Rhododendron
DRYING WITH SILICA GEL	Anemone • Azalea • Daisy • Freesia Lily of the Valley • Marigold • Orchid Pansy • Peony • Queen Anne's lace Rose • Zinnia
MICROWAVE DRYING	Buttercup • Chrysanthemum • Daffodil Delphinium • Gerbera daisy • Hydrangea Larkspur • Lilac • Pansy • Rose • Tulip • Zinnia

RESOURCES

DOMESTIC RESOURCES

MARIEMONT FLORIST, INC.

7257 Wooster Pike

Cincinnati, OH 45227

(800) 437-3567

www.mariemontflorist.com

Contact author, general information and assistance.

BOTANIQUE PRESERVATION EQUIPMENT, INC.

16610 N 25th Ave., Ste. 101

Phoenix, AZ 85023

(602) 9993-3364

www.botaniquefrzdry.com

Information on flower preservation and freeze drying.

C.M. OFFRAY & SON, INC.

360 Route 24

Chester, NJ 07930

(800) 551-LION

www.offray.com

Manufacturer of decorative ribbons.

DESIGN MASTER COLOR TOOL INC.

P.O. Box 601

Boulder, CO 80306

(303) 443-5214

www.dmcolor.com

Manufacturer of floral color sprays, paints and tints.

FLORACRAFT

One Longfellow Place

P.O. Box 400

Ludington, MI 49431

(616) 845-0240

www.floracraft.com

Manufacturer of floral sheet foam and general floral supplies.

FLORIST DIRECTORY

www.eflorist.com

Web directory to assist in finding a florist in your area.

FREEZEFRAME

6216 Hoke Road

Clayton, OH 45315

(937) 837-2389

www.freezeframeit.com

Provider of freeze-drying services.

JOHN HENRY COMPANY

5800 Grand River Ave.

P.O. Box 17099

Lansing, MI 48901-7099

(800) 968-5646

www.jhc.com

Leaf shine, floral preservatives and other floral supplies.

OASIS FLORAL PRODUCTS

P.O. Box 118

Kent, OH 44240

(800) 321-82286

Provider of floral foam products.

KNUD NIELSEN COMPANY, INC.

P.O. Box 746

Evergreen, AL 36401

Supplier of dried flowers and foliage.

SOCIETY OF AMERICAN FLORISTS

1601 Duke St.

Alexandria, VA 22314

(800) 336-4743

www.safnow.org

Resource for general information about the floral industry.

VABAN RIBBON

165 Eighth St.

San Francisco, CA 94103

(800) 448-9988

Provider of decorative ribbons.

INTERNATIONAL RESOURCES

FLORAL ART MALL

21/262 Centerway Rd.

Orewa

New Zealand

+64 9427 5681

www.floralartmall.com

Retailer of fresh and silk flowers, florist supplies and books.

INDEX

The best in floral inspiration and guidance is from North Light Books!

Wreaths for Every Season

Here are 20 beautiful wreath projects, perfect for brightening up a doorway or celebrating a special time of year. You'll find a range of sizes and styles, utilizing a variety of creative materials including dried herbs, sea shells, cinnamon sticks, silk flowers, autumn leaves, Christmas candy and more. Clear, step-by-step instructions ensure beautiful, long lasting results every time!

ISBN 1-58180-239-0, paperback, 144 pages, #32015-K

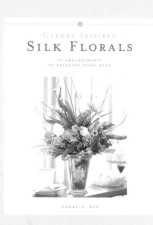

Garden-Inspired Silk Florals

Beautify your home with gorgeous silk floral arrangements that look as if they've just been picked fresh from the garden. Terry Rye presents 17 arrangements, complete with her expert tips, variation suggestions and materials lists. From Victorian-inspired urns and beautiful bulb compositions to sumptuous wreaths, swags and topiaries, you'll find a plethora of stunning ideas to bring the look of fresh garden flowers to your décor.

ISBN 1-58180-282-X, paperback, 128 pages, #32150-K

Fantastic Wreaths with Dale Rohman

America's flower man Dale Rohman shows you how to add elegance and personality to any room, door or occasion with these 20 fantastic wreath and garland projects. Each unique design includes easy-to-follow instructions, simple techniques, step-by-step photos and special tips that ensure gorgeous results every time. Dale uses a variety of materials to create each piece, including fresh roses, lemons, sunflowers, shells, ribbons, bamboo and more. Start today and keep your home stylish and welcoming all year long!

ISBN 1-58180-289-7, paperback, 128 pages, #32165-K

These books and other fine North Light craft titles are available from your local art & craft retailer, bookstore, online supplier or by calling 1-800-448-0915.